# LEGENDS AND HAUNTINGS
## OF THE
# JERSEY BAYSHORE

GOTHIC AMERICANA

# LEGENDS AND HAUNTINGS OF THE JERSEY BAYSHORE

## GREG CAGGIANO

FONTHILL

*To my friend Jeff. Thanks for everything.*

Fonthill Media Inc.
www.fonthillmedia.com
office@fonthillmedia.com

First published 2024



ISBN 978-1-62545-136-1



Typeset in 10pt on 13pt Sabon
Printed and bound in England

# ACKNOWLEDGMENTS

I have had the pleasure of investigating with an innumerable number of people over the years. This is between my own team members across two different groups, friends who have joined in, and co-investigating with other paranormal teams, and members of the public at various events. It is impossible to acknowledge everyone. Therefore, I have included names within the bodies of these chapters. If someone is specifically mentioned, it is because they either had an impact on the moment or provided me with a distinct memory that made it into this book with countless others needing to be omitted for brevity. To mention someone by name, in this book, is their acknowledgement. However, there are a few people who stand out as particularly important to the development of both this work and my own documenting of paranormal experiences and legends which precipitated its publishing.

Jeff Huber, my former history professor turned dear friend, who got me to be involved in historical interpretation at the Proprietary House Museum where I became their youngest ever trustee at age eighteen. It was here that I was able to develop and hone my skills as a historian and also a paranormal investigator. Jeff was a kind and knowledgeable soul who would do anything for a friend. Our paranormal adventures were not extensive, but they were important enough that without them, I might not be the same person I am today. Jeff sadly and unexpectedly passed away in 2020 at age fifty-three. Reminiscing about our brief time together was one of my favorite parts of writing this book, which I have dedicated to his memory.

Patty Bickauskas, who is the EVP expert of our group Ghosts on the Coast. Without her diligence, patience, and attention to detail, our record of evidence would be sorely lacking. She is the one who takes hours of audio and listens to them for the slightest hint of a ghostly whisper. In addition, she is also an excellent researcher who has delved into newspaper archives in order to assist me in finding missing information I needed to either prove or debunk various stories and legends. She was particularly helpful for research in sections pertaining to Whipporwill Road and the Dempsey House. She is also a board member and tireless volunteer at the Strauss Mansion Museum, where I have also served, making it accessible for paranormal research to groups from far and wide.

Patrick Osborn, our group's principal videographer. He has helped visually document many of the experiences described in this book. Just like I was a student of Jeff and became friends, Patrick was once my student who became my friend. He began volunteering at historic sites with me while in high school and eventually joined our paranormal team. He has now graduated college, and in addition to making me feel old, has become vital in helping analyze SB-7 Spirit Box recordings. He painstakingly plays, replays, slows down, and speeds up audio and video footage to try to best capture our "conversations" with the other side. This book would not be the same without his help.

I also wish to thank Josh Greenland at Fonthill for his assistance with the editing of this book, as well as my friend and lifelong Bayshore resident Jamie McGlaughlin for her proofreading and feedback.

# CONTENTS

# THE LEGENDARY COASTLINE OF THE JERSEY BAYSHORE

Somehow, New Jersey always gets a bad rap. It is the target of jokes and never quite taken seriously by the rest of the country. But what we really have is an incredibly rich history that much of the country cannot come close to. The specific area discussed in this book is known as the "Bayshore." This is the northern part of the famed "Jersey Shore." It begins in the Perth Amboy and Woodbridge area at the mouth of the Raritan River and then curves along Raritan Bay towards Highlands and Sandy Hook. It contains over thirty towns, both directly on the water and a short distance inland. Not every town will be explored in this book, for reasons which you will soon read.

For as much of the history that is well known, there is an equal part that people will be surprised to read about. The list is endless, and contains something for everyone. Whether it is the Lenape Indians, European explorers, soldiers of the American Revolution or World War II, pirates, espionage, murders and true crime, bootleggers and gangsters, and secret underground passageways, it may be impossible to fathom that all of these events and incidents occurred in what is a relatively small area over the course of 300 years.

I have woven in personal stories of the paranormal as well as established legends and lore with the history. I am a historian first, and a paranormal investigator second. So, while I feel the need to compile a list of stories that are interesting, I also need to explain and debunk them when need be. This is a comprehensive approach that gives you multiple sides to the same stories and locations.

## "LEGEND HAS IT…"

Even the most outlandish and obviously untrue legends still deserve documentation in the historical record because they reflect the intrinsic belief system of a particular locale or stories that have been incorporated into the lore of a specific house or building. The stories told from one generation to another to either frighten, warn, or intrigue. The abandoned house at the corner. The witch in the woods. The more well-known Jersey Devil. That is what fascinates me: where did they start? All legends seem to have a root or origin.

As an avid lifelong reader of *Weird N.J.*, I look at the importance of this biannual magazine publication as not just entertainment, but a documentation of such stories into our New Jersey culture. Some of the Bayshore locations featured over the years pop up in this book. While more often than not, I have to prove them to not be true because I value the history above all else, they are still crucial because they sometimes show the evolution of a simple tale into something unable to be contained, and most importantly, demonstrate what people have believed and how there can be many different versions of the same basic tale. *Weird N.J.* may be the most important publication in the history of pop culture and belief systems in the Garden State.

Though not associated with the Bayshore, the story of the Jersey Devil is a prime example of how something probably mundane or at least explainable exploded into what we have today. It has been my opinion for many years that Mrs. Leeds (always labeled the "mother" of the creature) did in fact give birth to something on the night that would change folklore history. However, being in the early 1700s and lacking proper medical care and diagnoses, and living in a strict religious and superstitious society where every good thing that happened to you was from God and everything bad from the Devil, she probably gave birth to a deformed child which those present as witnesses could not comprehend or explain.

Maybe the child had a cleft palate. Maybe a tail-bone protruding out of its backside, now known medically as a pseudotail which is an extremely rare but certainly possible symptom of spina bifida. While both can be cured today through surgeries, three centuries ago the sufferer would have been entirely out of luck. From this deformed child no doubt came stories of evil-doing on behalf of the Leeds family (who are referred to as witches by some sources), and ever since, people have "seen things" in the Pine Barrens area of southern New Jersey.

The Bayshore has no shortage of legends associated with buildings and areas. While not as grand as a human giving birth to a monster that literally flew out of the womb and haunted an entire region for hundreds of years, they are interesting enough to be included in this book. There are tales of murders, suicide, witchcraft, and clandestine ritualistic activities. Some of these stories have a clear foundation and origin, and regardless of how inane they may seem today, we can at least trace where they came from and understand why. Then there are others that come from absolutely nowhere.

My job as a historian who happens to investigate these topics is to use historical knowledge of this particular region and apply it to each case without getting caught up in how "cool" it would be if such stories were true. Then there are the murders and incidents which really did occur and managed to slip into obscurity and away from most people except the ardent history nerds out there.

## COMPILING THE EVIDENCE

In terms of the paranormal, which is more tangible than a legend since it can hopefully be documented through various means of technology and firsthand eyewitness accounts, I make sure to differentiate between experiences that I personally lived through *versus* ones that have long been associated with a particular property or were relayed to me over years researching in the field and talking to people.

Finding the historical or folklore information came via a number of mediums, such as books, magazine and newspaper articles, vintage newspaper databases, and internet blogs and websites. The latter two might not normally be acceptable in a history book, but because they give insight into what people believe and can show how a story may spread, taking many different shapes, they are vital even if not true.

Some popular legends and stories will be debunked while others remain open-ended. It is hard to "prove" anything regarding a paranormal experience, because although I am a believer in a life of some kind after death, I must remain skeptical—not just of stories told to me but events I have witnessed myself. There always might be another cause other than the supernatural, which is usually excitement or momentary fear causing human error or misjudgment.

I have talked to many people over the years. Hosting various fundraising paranormal events for the last decade has put me in contact with a wide array of individuals who want to share their stories. I have determined that only an infinitesimal amount of people lie to create a scenario. Most are either mistaken and truly believe the incident they experienced was paranormal. One of those people will be me in the last chapter of this book, when I tell you of an incredible moment captured on camera that ended up being nothing more than a technological anomaly.

Whether lecturing on this subject as I have done for years or writing this book, my job is not to sell or prove anything to you, but to give you the information and descriptions (and hard evidence when possible) at my disposal so you may form your own opinion.

Believers will believe, skeptics will question, and the devout non-believers will dismiss. Regardless of which category you fall under, I think everyone will be fascinated by the history seen in these ghostly or macabre tales. Readers of all kinds will be interested in the evolution of a legend, or in the case of a paranormal experience I believe to be totally genuine, still trying to figure out an ulterior explanation. As an educator, if anything I write gets you to think critically, explore a location for yourself, or investigate a topic further, I will have done my job.

There may be evidence to back up paranormal experiences, but there will never be proof. Not provided by me. Not provided by anybody. Simply put, the paranormal is impossible to prove. No matter how authentic a story might be, there is the possibility for doubt and human error. If something is captured on camera, there will always be the chance that it is an innocent mistake, something was overlooked, or possibly fabricated. So many investigators waste time trying to prove, when such a belief can never be forced.

There is, however, one item that makes this book different from so many other regional ghost story or folklore collections out there, and that is there are plenty of moments described within these chapters that are captured on camera and are available for viewing on the YouTube channel for the paranormal group I am a part of: Ghosts on the Coast. Some are audio recordings and others contain video of actual suspected paranormal activity. In these instances, you do not have to determine whether or not you can take my word for it, but you can look up the videos (via a reference list provided at the end of the book) and see them for yourself. Unfortunately, not every incident is on this channel, because many moments described occurred when we were not filming or at a location working.

## THE LOCATIONS

There may be places in the Bayshore area that people were expecting to be in this book that are not. Possibly some obvious choices. I assure you that none of them were intentionally ignored or overlooked. This book is my own personal journey into the paranormal and studying various myths and legends that began in 2009 and continues now in 2024. This book is essentially a memoir and recounts nearly fifteen years of experiences, moments, and events. This is a journal of such activities as they came and went in my life, and some places just happened to not cross that path.

I wrote one book in 2014 which was published by the Atlantic Highlands Historical Society. It was a collection of only one year's worth of paranormal investigations at the Strauss Mansion, their headquarters, where I had recently begun volunteering and investigating frequently. Those moments were intentionally written down with the goal of getting a book published about them clearly in mind.

The making of this current book was not so standard. I had compiled years' worth of research, notes, and accounts for my own personal knowledge and also to craft lectures about them to a wide variety of audiences. In a given year, I may present anywhere from ten to twenty lectures on the paranormal, folklore, and the occult, most occurring in October. Then there are the incidents captured on camera. I, and the majority of my team, are in over 200 videos on YouTube spanning the last ten years or so. While I had always planned on writing a sequel, and had assembled copious notes, it never happened due to publishing costs.

The museum took a chance and agreed to pay for the first one, and in turn, I agreed to write it for free. It was a trade-off that I have never regretted, as it gave me the chance to have a book published. However, due to such financial constraints, a lot was edited out of the book to shorten it. Then, as it happened, right after the book was published, we had some amazing experiences that occurred a little too late to matter. Looking back on it now, the only thing I wish I had done differently was wait—and wait for several years so I had more to write about, and the chance to have fundraised more money for its publication. The book still sells at the Mansion's gift shop, and I was told a couple of years after publication that enough copies were sold to cover the cost. I never wanted to ask for such a favor, another book, again. Because so much has happened since, both there and numerous other exciting places, and I have seen my own evolution as a writer, I try to pretend that the first book does not exist.

My notes became just for me and my lecture audiences with their eventual use for a book seeming slimmer and slimmer. How this book came to be was something I never expected. The publisher of Fonthill saw me telling ghost stories in a video. No, not one of 200 on YouTube which have been seen by tens of thousands of people, but on an obscure special features vignette for a 2016 Blu-Ray of a horror movie that was filmed at the Strauss Mansion in 1979 which I was asked to participate in. As fate would have it, I was asked about writing a book about my experiences, and to not just include this location, but as many as I wanted. I decided to make it about places in the Jersey Bayshore, so they would at least have a common theme and all be relatively close to one another in proximity.

Thus, I had never sought to research for the sake of writing a book. The personal experiences and research had already been compiled, though I did end up exploring more sources when one item led to another (for some of the locations) as I put it in narrative form. This book is a byproduct of that. Every building or site is integral to my journey, and not "thrown in" just because it seemed like it was necessary. It needed to have a special meaning to me and is why some places may seem left out. This is another area where my book differs from so many regional books about ghosts and legends. There are hundreds, if not thousands in print across the country. Not to sound arrogant, but I have not read any of the ones pertaining to the area of New Jersey in which I live, though I will read books about other places.

This has to be so, because as I am giving my many lectures about these locations, I do not need anyone else's stories creeping into my mind. They need to be what I either went through myself, was told firsthand by someone else, or documented as part of established lore. I took that same approach to this book, using other accounts only when absolutely necessary to build a case and also show what people have believed, not that I personally believe them. I hope the authors of those books understand, just as I would if they did not want to read this one for the same reason. Some of these places, such as the Proprietary House and Spy House, have already been written about by others. Most of them, though, have never made it into such a book, and I am confident that even the most devoted consumer of paranormal literature will still be able to find something fresh and new here.

This book is not going to recount the same chilling yet tired tales you have already heard with no explanation offered for their existence. It is about my team and I immersing ourselves into the subject matter and trying to investigate the truth. In most cases, legends are debunked. This is not done with any joy to ruin someone's day. It is done to stay as close to the reality of a situation as possible. In some cases, there is truth to be found, and perhaps where least expected. In others, the truth is more bizarre than any fictional creation.

I was lucky enough to serve on the boards of two museums which were haunted: the Proprietary House in Perth Amboy, where I volunteered from 2009 to 2013 and was a trustee for three of those years, and the Atlantic Highlands Historical Society, which is housed at the Strauss Mansion, where I have been since 2013, and was on the board of directors for eight years. This gave me unrivaled access to two exceptionally haunted locations, and is why the chapters which serve as the bookends are the longest and most detailed. I did not get involved at either place for the paranormal. It was for history, with ghostly interest coming later.

I do not want anyone to get the false impression of two things: 1) that these museums are "haunted house" attractions, and 2) that such paranormal activity is so easily captured. Both are working museums, each dedicated to a particular time period and genre which happen to be haunted. Also, the only reason for so many stories is because of the amount of time I have spent at each place, not just investigating but simply volunteering or working in broad daylight. This is especially so at the Strauss Mansion, where I was much more active, serving on numerous committees and planning events. There were some times that I felt I was devoting more time to them than my real jobs. That is why I have so many stories.


## THE TEAM

Since I started investigating, I have been a part of two groups: Haunted Travels from 2013–2015, which I co-founded with my friend Jake Reid, and then Ghosts on the

Coast from 2015 to present, which was founded along with another friend Brett Bodner. In just those two years, we managed to acquire better cameras and equipment, which led to better evidence being discovered. Team members have come and gone and come back again. Both groups ended up containing the same people because we truly are like family. We got caught up in this through our volunteering at historic sites, whether it be the Proprietary House or the Strauss Mansion. In fact, by the time Ghosts on the Coast got through a few seasons worth of videos and started establishing itself, every single member of our team was either on the board of directors of the Strauss Mansion or an active volunteer.

Almost all of us started in this field because of a love of history. It also gave us a chance to meet different people, and host them for paranormal events. This allowed our group to also investigate along with other groups and work together. The Strauss Mansion became our unofficial headquarters where we could use what we do to bring in much-needed fundraising. Every video we filmed there was potential advertising for other people to see it and say, "I want to visit that place!" In recent years, our EVP expert Patty Bickauskas (the only member of our team to join for the ghosts and end up becoming a board member, not the other way around) has coordinated rentals of the Strauss Mansion where groups can come in after-hours and dig around for themselves.

In getting back to our channel, over the years we have had no problems posting footage from investigations that did not capture any evidence at all. We have all felt the need to be "real" with people and also educate them on what it is like to take part in an investigation. This is not television or the movies. No matter how haunted a place may be, or how many experiences we may have had there previously, there are some nights where you simply come up empty-handed. We have purposefully kept our channel free of sponsors and committed to the mindset that a fruitless investigation can be a learning experience or just downright fun. If this book was a movie, there would be a blooper reel. Many times we have left a location and were able to say, "Well, we did not get anything tonight." Such an authenticity is why I have always enjoyed working with the people you will meet in this book.

## THE EQUIPMENT

No one on our team is a psychic or medium or any other term for someone that can interact with the dead on their own or "see things." This is for the simple reason that when doing investigations for the express reason of being able to lecture about them or give fundraiser tours at a haunted location, we prefer to be able to show visitors something concrete, such as a shadow movement captured on camera or audio on a tape recorder of a ghost speaking to us, not just "A psychic here once saw…" If someone feels a cold spot by them, we turn to technological instruments that will hopefully corroborate what the person is experiencing.

Of course, not everything can be captured by devices, but telling people what we ourselves experienced just like any normal person would lends some sanity to a field that has become overrun with attention seekers. None of us in our group have any special ability. The only time psychics will be referenced is when documenting previously existing stories at a site or when interacting with outside groups who brought one along.

I do not mean for that to sound like a condemnation of people professing to be psychic. I believe there are some people out there who genuinely have an ability of some kind. But if you put yourself in my shoes, working with too many groups to count, and meeting a number of psychics over the years who so confidently told us information right to our faces that we knew was provably false, you would understand my skepticism. This is why knowing the history of a location inside and out is so important.

The only non-technological activity we participate in is something called a "Wine Glass Séance." It is similar to a Ouija board, and people certainly have mixed feelings on them. We first began doing these at the Strauss Mansion, since this was a Victorian-era method of contacting the dead and the building dated to that time period. None of us were expecting it to work, but it did. So long as everyone honestly rests their finger on the upside-down wine glass (which acts as a planchette and moves within a circle of letters) and does not do anything to move it, it will work.

If everyone is genuine, and it moves, there might be something there. Skeptics will probably not allow for belief in this method, for even if they believe that no one on the team is moving the glass, it has been said by experts that it is being done unconsciously or the work of the subconscious mind. This may be so, but we have had interesting results in finding out information that none of us knew previously. We do not use this method at every investigation, only when we begin to grow bored with some of our other techniques.

We rely on several pieces of technology to attempt to communicate with ghosts at haunted locations and also try to document whether or not they are around us at a particular time. Many references to such equipment will be throughout this book and can be seen in our YouTube videos.

The first and most prominent is the SB-7 Spirit Box. I will refer to this as either the "SB-7" or "Spirit Box" to prevent overuse of the word. This is a small radio that scans AM or FM radio stations at a rate of up to ten per second. It creates a loud static sound known as white noise. Within this noise is the chance to sometimes hear actual ghostly communication. There is no telling why our group, and hundreds of others, have found this to work. People who do not believe in it will say that the words are just from the radio or noises being mistaken for words. While I will allow that single word responses may not be paranormal, if the device is set to sweep at its highest rate, the radio would not be on a station long enough to hear a word, especially not a complete sentence as we have heard many times.

Most of the "conversations" in this book are through the SB-7. Others are from electronic voice phenomena (EVP), which is when a voice is captured on a tape or audio recorder. These are a more conclusive form of evidence and much harder to acquire. Not just because it takes the spirit an enormous amount of energy to be heard (though our ears may not hear it), but the energy it takes the investigator to sift through hours of recordings. This is what Patty has done for us. While we routinely post excellent EVPs, it is not because they are easy to get or that we are better than anyone else. In reality, Patty may listen to a five-hour audio clip in the hopes to just hear a couple of words over a few seconds. She has to filter through our own voices and background noises to hear those usually slight whispers. It seems like we have a lot, but we just have someone with the patience to do the listening.

Helpful to us in recent years has been a trap camera, which is normally used outdoors by hunters to track wild game. This camera can be mounted in an area of a building where we are not going to be walking by. It starts filming only when triggered by motion, and will take still photographs, or if there is prolonged movement, a thirty-second video clip. The battery can last for days. With our access to the Strauss Mansion, we will often leave it there overnight when no one is in the building to see if any ghosts might be lurking around. The results at several of these placements have been astounding.

As for determining energy and movement, we have several K-2 and EMF meters which both detect changes in the electromagnetic field, such as if an entity is nearby. There is also a Mel-Meter that displays the temperature in addition to energy levels, which is important to have on hand if someone is experiencing a cold spot. The technology has increased drastically and for the better in recent years. There is now an EMF "trip wire" which is 36 feet long and can be laid on the floor or hung up. We usually position this going down a staircase or on the floor to see if anything is coming towards us. This is our most recent addition, and have limited experiences with it.

## FINAL WORD BEFORE OUR JOURNEY

These chapters are not really in a chronological order, with the exception of the first and last. All the other ones in between bounce around anywhere from 2009 until present day. I have tried to group them more for their eras in history rather than my own investigating. The available equipment at our disposal changes based on what year it was. For the chapter on the Proprietary House, we had hardly anything, whereas by the time we get to the Strauss Mansion, there are all kinds of modern equipment being used to capture evidence.

All of the locations are less than an hour away from each other, most within only twenty minutes. It is therefore possible to do a road trip based on this book, stopping at each one in a single day. Several of them are open to the public but with limited hours, some are outdoors and open year-round for exploration, and others may be closed off but are at least visible from public property.

In more than a decade of investigating and lecturing, I have tried to make this field as accessible as possible. I am not an expert, merely someone who just has a lot of experience. I think you will find that this book can be enjoyed by believers and skeptics alike, as I have found with my presentations that deal with some of the same ideas. Anyone can do what my group and I do. We have also made sure to share our locations with others, as the Strauss Mansion is now a popular place to investigate when it was not so much before I got involved. That is what this should be about: our researching of myths and legends, and our paranormal investigations should all seek the truth, and everyone should be able to share their findings rather than compete or close off places to others. Unfortunately, there is usually little collaboration, depending on who the groups are, and people are desperate to hold onto stories that they have heard their whole life.

This book will confirm a lot of what you know and shock you with what you do not. This was also a learning experience for me, as finally cataloging years' worth of information and events in one place was eye-opening, and I was there myself. I hope you enjoy the journey.

# 1

# THE HAUNTING OF THE ROYAL GOVERNOR'S MANSION

## PROPRIETARY HOUSE, PERTH AMBOY

The Proprietary House in Perth Amboy spoiled me early on as a paranormal investigator. Long established as one of the most haunted buildings in New Jersey, if not the entire United States, it was quite a location to have my introduction into both the fields of the paranormal and also historical interpretation at such a young age. I had started as a volunteer there in 2009 and was quickly asked to join the Board of Trustees as an eighteen-year-old, since I had knowledge of computers and social media, and was tasked with trying to bring the museum into the next century via a better website and online communication with the public. A history professor of mine and also the official historian for neighboring Woodbridge, Jeff Huber, had become a good friend by then, and he was on the executive board. There was perhaps no greater influence in my life at the time than Jeff, as he gave me my start in two areas that define who I am today.

As my professor, he had arranged for a trip for my freshman history class to visit the former residence of New Jersey's last royal governor (and patriot Founding Father Benjamin's son), William Franklin. While the trip was for Revolutionary War history purposes, the question of whether or not the place was haunted assuredly came up. We then were told numerous ghost stories, some of which are quite famous and are repeated by various people and sources today. Jeff offered the chance for any of us to join him there one night for a ghost hunt. Only I and three others answered the call. It was November 2009, and it was a night that would change my life forever.

No, we did not discover any incredible evidence. The few experiences we had were mundane, but the mere act of calling into the darkness to see if anything would respond was thrilling. As a lifelong history lover, this was a chance to reach out into the past and communicate with someone who had lived before me.

As I gradually became a volunteer and later a trustee, I was made aware of the many paranormal experiences and ghost stories to occur at the Proprietary House over the years. We held ghost tours every October led by a well-known psychic. During each tour, she would guide people around the house giving a running commentary of what she was

17

seeing—you can liken it to a sports "play by play." I never knew exactly what to make of the individual, since each tour was nearly the same as the one before it.

The basement kitchen, which was next to what most people considered the front door (even though the main entrance in Franklin's time was on the next side of the house), served as the waiting room for the tours. Whether this psychic was legitimate or not, people loved the tours. Some years, there was a line down the street waiting to get in. Myself and a few volunteers would keep the waiting guests entertained with additional stories.

The oldest involves the Perth Amboy police department arriving to tell whoever the caretaker or docent was at the time to remove mannequins from the windows, as they were distracting to drivers who were coming down Kearny Avenue. Supposedly, numerous people had been so startled or distracted by faces or bodily shapes staring at them out from the windows on that side of the building that they swerved or nearly got into a collision.

By my estimation, this story was at least twenty years old at the time, making it stem from the late 1980s or early '90s, which was the peak of ghost tour activity at the Proprietary House. As widely known and eye-opening as this story is, it may be apocryphal in nature—someone seeing or thinking they saw something and then telling someone else and like a game of telephone from one person to the next exploded into an incident so severe that the police had to be called, and arrived only to be told that there are not, nor ever were, mannequins in the museum at all, much less placed spookily by the windows.

I only ever had two interactions with the local police department in my four years volunteering, both while doing late night investigations with fellow trustees and their friends and family. Someone had called the cops because they saw people moving around the house with flashlights and thought there was a burglary in progress. Both times when the officers arrived, I opened the door and Jeff and I would show our keys and say who we are. We always asked if they wanted to come in, and in each instance, the cops hurried jokingly away saying, "No thank you!" It is good that we were not really robbing the place.

Right by where this figure was said to be seen was another window on the first floor in what is now the colonial dining room, where people routinely stood in front of and felt disoriented. A caretaker of the Proprietary House before it was a state-operated museum (no year was given, but likely in the 1960s) died in that very spot, which was his bedroom at the time. He was supposedly a severe alcoholic who died with a whiskey bottle in his possession. Some versions claimed he had only one arm. From then on out, visitors would feel his drunkenness by standing in the area where he died. We later realized that the floorboards by the window were uneven, and judging by how someone stood there might have made those more sensitive to an equilibrium imbalance feel uneasy or that they would fall over. This story does have basis in truth, as a long-time volunteer who I knew then was the person who found the gentleman's body. He also added that there was a cigarette still in his hand, next to the whiskey bottle. We should all go out that way.

The many uses of the Proprietary House over the years may be the reason why its haunting stands out in a state with an endless array of creepy houses. It was built in 1762 by Scottish architect John Edward Pryor to serve as the residence for New

Jersey's royal governor while the colonies were still under British rule. While Franklin became governor in 1763, it was not until 1774 that he moved into this house. He then lived there for nearly two years until his fateful arrest in June 1776 at the hands of a militia colonel, Nathanial Heard from Woodbridge, under the direction of the Provincial Congress of New Jersey. Since January of that year, he had been placed under house arrest for his loyalty to King George III, whom he admired and wanted to continue serving.

He was ordered to not conduct any government business, but instead, secretly plotted with agents of the crown. When this was discovered by the Congress, he had to be removed. Heard initially arrived under orders to treat Franklin with respect and try to coerce him one last time before a full arrest. Franklin was so insulted at who was chosen for the assignment that he refused to speak to him. According to popular legend, Franklin spun around on his heel and slammed the door in Heard's face. When Heard arrived a second time, it was with a militia and much more forceful. Previously, between January and June of that year, Benjamin and William passionately argued for their causes, neither able to find common ground or sway the opinion of the other.

In one of the greatest break-ups in American history, in a war that saw so many towns, regions, and families in New Jersey split between either patriot or loyalist feelings, William chose to remain loyal to the British, referring to the new government as an "illegal assembly," while his father became an ardent patriot and one of the most beloved figures in our history.

William was his illegitimate son who Benjamin raised as his own with common-law wife Deborah Read. At a time when someone in William's position would have been seen as a "bastard," he lived quite a successful life and was beloved in New Jersey almost until the very end. He has essentially been written out of history because of his refusal to switch sides during the American Revolution. He is so unknown that while volunteering there, I would not tell people I worked at William Franklin's house. Instead, I phrased it as "Benjamin Franklin's son's house" so they would have an idea of what I was talking about. However, though many people do not know of his story, we have all seen him before. In the famous painting of Benjamin experimenting with electricity by flying a kite with a key during a thunderstorm, there is a little boy accompanying him. That boy was William.

Following his arrest, he would be imprisoned for two years in Connecticut before returning to New York where he would continue to support the crown by rallying loyalists and organizing acts of violence against patriots there as well as in New Jersey. Franklin's involvement in the Bayshore area will return in the next chapter of this book, when we examine another location and how fractured this area was during the Revolution.

His arrest in 1776 occurred at the front door of the Proprietary House, just off the foyer and drawing room. This is an event that is reenacted annually in June by the museum, and something I took part in several times as a volunteer in Heard's militia—I had the opportunity to direct one year. It is done right on the very spot where it occurred, adding to the realism of this dramatic event. William's wife, Elizabeth Downes, witnessed the arrest and would never see him again, as she died heartbroken two years later while he was still in prison. William lived until 1813, dying in England while in exile, never reconciling with Benjamin, though they did meet one last time to settle legal issues. His father got the final word when in his last will and testament, he addressed him:

> To my son, William Franklin, late Governor of the Jerseys, I give and devise all the lands I hold or have a right to, in the province of Nova Scotia, to hold to him, his heirs, and assigns forever. I also give to him all my books and papers, which he has in his possession, and all debts standing against him on my account books, willing that no payment for, nor restitution of, the same be required of him, by my executors. The part he acted against me in the late war, which is of public notoriety, will account for my leaving him no more of an estate he endeavored to deprive me of.

In hindsight, most people tend to side with Benjamin without much thought because we grow up with a hazy understanding of all patriots being good and all loyalists being bad. But does anyone take the time to understand William? This includes his own father who dismissed his son's convictions despite having a reputable and popular political career and refused to attempt to see his side of the story. In this they could have still maintained friendly terms through disagreement. But under the patriotic fervor encapsulating the situation, the reaction was anger and ignorance, not amicable and forgiving. Ironically enough, had the British won the Revolution as expected initially, it would be William with monuments, namesakes, and celebratory triumph, not Benjamin.

This all caused myriad emotions to hover over the Proprietary House. There have been numerous reports over the years of people seeing a "Lady in White" walking the halls. Many haunted locations have similar tales of the spirit of a sad woman who is usually either waiting for a long-lost husband to return or knowing the husband is dead and is unable to move on, still mourning him. While such a figure is synonymous with a "Lady in White," they are not necessarily wearing white every time. The figure at this house is usually seen in fleeting glimpses, and is alleged to be William's wife, as she went through the trauma of not only seeing him arrested but never seeing him again at all.

A female spirit of unknown identity was seen by a visitor or, in some versions of the story, a Comcast technician who went to the wrong area of the house (aside from the museum on the bottom two floors, there is office space in the above floors rented out by the state and also a second building on the property built in the 1800s) who managed to get into the house when it was closed and some volunteers were upstairs. They heard footsteps coming from the basement up to the first floor and were surprised to see this man walking in so nonchalantly and asked how he got in. The volunteers were then told that the basement door was open and there was a costumed interpreter in the office (which is by that door) who invited him in and said he was welcome to go upstairs. Of course, there was no interpreter present and when they told this person what must have transpired, he quickly left.

It is hard to determine whether this really happened, though it was within the few years prior to me getting involved in 2009. I spoke to three different trustees after first hearing this and each offered a different variation of the same basic story. Whatever the case may be, it is within the realm of possibility, though I personally have never seen a full-bodied spirit so casually with my own eyes like this person did. Indeed, one afternoon, when the museum was closed and I was with a few volunteers—including our president at the time, Thomas Ward—doing some painting, a man did manage to enter through the same basement door and come up the stairs and ask for a tour. Despite being closed, we gave him one. We all swore we had locked the front door, but it was open, and he let himself in. Nothing paranormal occurred this time around.

The one recurring presence that I have somewhat of a firsthand account of is the story of the "Boy in Blue," who has been seen by workers and visitors alike for decades. He is referred to as this because he is about ten years old and wears an old-fashioned outfit that is entirely blue. He had been nicknamed "Alexander" by the time I arrived, and several paranormal groups and psychics had experiences with him previously. During one investigation, I witnessed an investigator sit on the floor and call for Alexander. He rolled a ball, and it stopped rather suddenly in the middle of the floor and rolled back. Further attempts were not replicated. They then tried a toy car, which also failed, and prompted Jeff to quip, "Well, he wouldn't really know what a car is, would he?"

Jeff's niece, Karli Huber, reported seeing the boy this evening, before the investigation had started and before she knew the story or anything about the spirit. She was of a similar age and saw a boy in strange blue clothing enter one of the rooms in the basement. Excited to see someone her own age, she proceeded after him only to find there was no one in the room. She thought, perhaps, he was a child of one of the investigators who had brought him along for the night. At a living history event the next year, where I was part of a military timeline and dressed like a Revolutionary War soldier, I was asked by a visitor if "that boy" was my younger brother and how nice it was to see young people involved in history. I was perplexed, with the thought of our ghostly friend not being on my mind. I said, "Who?" and she said, "The kid in blue." Not wanting to get into who he was or trying to tell this woman that there are no young children present, I just said that he was not my brother.

The Proprietary House had an elevator installed sometime in the 1980s, and any time it would malfunction, workers would blame it on Alexander who a visiting psychic had said enjoyed riding it. If this was not true, it was a way to have fun with an elevator unpredictable enough that even someone with a broken leg would probably prefer the stairs. *News 12 New Jersey*, in a Halloween-themed featurette, sent one of their reporters into the "haunted elevator" in 2011 or 2012 hoping to have an experience. As expected, nothing happened.

Another tale told to me was of a postman with a package who sought one of the offices upstairs and knocked on the basement door of the museum when it was closed only to be met by a little boy who the man assumed was a child of one of the workers. The boy not only led him to the elevator but got on with him, pushed the buttons to get him upstairs, and when the man entered the correct floor and turned around to thank him, he was gone. Such a story had been told over and over again to the point that it did not matter if it was true because it was good and people loved hearing it.

But who was this boy and where did he come from? Possible explanations are endless, as for any spirit at the Proprietary House since the building had many uses following Franklin's arrest. Oddly enough, at no time did we ever think we communicated with the governor, nor do I have stories from anyone else (to my knowledge) that mention his ghost being there though it is automatically assumed. And that would make sense, considering that he spent less than two years of his eighty-three on this earth at the Proprietary House.

Following his and his family's removal, it was owned by a British secret agent, John Rattoone, and then in the 1800s by a merchant named Matthias Bruen, who was one of the wealthiest men in America. Aside from several private ownerships, it served as a hotel named The Brighton when a second building nearly equal in size was added, connected to the original structure. One additional floor was added above where Franklin lived. It also saw time as a retirement home for disabled Presbyterian ministers and their wives and orphans, a hospital for recovering officers during the American Civil War following the battle of Gettysburg, and an apartment building.

People hear "hospital" and "orphanage" and "retirement home" and immediately start to have eerie thoughts, since neither of the three conjure up happy images. Even with these potential fire-starters for all kinds of lurid stories, there really are none to offer—at least none that can be confirmed. And aside from only one or two negative experiences, I never felt threatened by anything at the Proprietary House.

As with psychics, some of whom are never satisfied with simply identifying a spirit, one visiting medium told us that Alexander was the son of a former caretaker in the 1800s who murdered him by pushing him out a window. By the end of the night, the story changed to that he was one of the orphans killed by the headmaster or whoever was in charge. None of this can be documented, nor do I believe it. I debated whether to include it in this book, but as I said in the introduction, it may be worth documenting to show what is believed at haunted locations and how a legend can fester.

Unfortunately, during more than a decade of investigating, I have not been so fortunate to see a full-bodied spirit. Alexander never appeared in stereotypical "see-through" form, as evidenced by the woman who possibly saw him at our reenactment event, but as an actual person standing in front of her. I have, however, seen shadows that moved in ways they should not have and, above all, have heard noises and strange anomalies.

I was at the Proprietary House from 2009 until 2013, and while it certainly was the right place, it was also the wrong time. This predates the founding of an actual paranormal group by my friends and I, who loosely referred to ourselves at the time as Haunted Travels. The investigative equipment we had at our disposal was also archaic compared to what we have available today.

For this reason, these experiences are not all physically recorded for one's viewing pleasure and review on YouTube like more recent investigations and videos that are referenced in future chapters. We had no light-up K-2 meters, no SB-7, and no FLIR or trap cameras. We had cameras that were not very good and tape recorders, and that was pretty much it. This chapter also lacks many of my own personal photos, which are simply not of a high enough quality to be published.

Visiting groups sometimes brought night-vision cameras which made us feel like we were on a TV show. But we never saw anything through them. For anyone that has done paranormal investigations for more than just the last five to seven years or so, they will agree with me when I say it is amazing how far we have come—that ten years ago, we were setting a twist-top flashlight down on a table and asking the ghosts to make it flicker as a sign of their presence and were over the moon if it did. Today, we would not waste time with such a method.

I may not have seen anything outstanding there, but I did hear three of the only four disembodied voices of my life at the Proprietary House. One night, three of us entered through the basement and made our way upstairs to the first floor. As I got to the top step and was about to enter the hallway, we all heard the thunderous sound of people laughing and having a commotion. It was so loud that my first thought was not paranormal, but to grab my phone and call the police because people had broken in and were having a party. We turned the light on and rushed toward the breakfast room, which is where the sound came from, flicked on another light, and saw absolutely nothing. This might have been the first time I was genuinely stunned by an occurrence. I, as well as the two others, Jake Reid (my first co-investigator along with Jeff) and his friend, could not help but stare at each other in a state of shock. We checked the rest of the museum, but there was nothing to find.

The other two times contained distinct words. I had met Jeff one evening to go over some information for the reenactment we were working on, and while sitting in the drawing room (which is where chairs were set up for the performance), we clearly heard a child's voice say, "Wanna play?" I immediately got up and went over to the window which overlooked the street. It was still light out and it would be easy to tell if anyone was around. There was no one there. We walked to the breakfast room which had a view of the parking lot where sometimes kids from the neighborhood hung out, and it was empty. The words clearly came from inside the house, but we had to make sure. The skeptic in me still has to allow for the possibility that it did come from outside, though we both know what we heard and reacted simultaneously, but it would be arrogant to profess to be so certain.

Lastly, during an afternoon with another one of our board members, Steve Probert, the phone rang, and it was from a lawyer's secretary who had an office in the old hotel/orphanage building. They were having computer trouble and wanted to know if anyone was there who could help. I never asked why they thought to call the museum, but we both went over. This was my first time inside that area.

Unless someone has been to the property, they may be entirely unaware of the existence of this second building. Somehow, despite being almost the same size and directly back and to the left of the Proprietary House if facing the front door, it manages to evade capture in most photographs of the museum. We made our way upstairs to either the second or third floor and found the office, which was small and had two desks: one for the lawyer who appeared to be in his eighties and another across the room for the secretary who could not have been much younger. He explained what was wrong with his computer, which was positioned in the corner on a separate table. He sat on a chair, Steve stood behind him looking over his shoulder, and I stood about 5 feet or so away, in front of his desk.

As Steve attempted to fix the problem, I heard the words, "Hello, I'm here, right here" spoken very quickly almost without pause between them. It sounded like a child's voice, high-pitched. Steve and I both reached for the phones in our pockets thinking we had accidentally called someone and they were trying to get our attention, but both of our phones were still on the lock screen. I said something to the effect of, "What was that?" and Steve just shook his head, trying to comprehend the situation. The lawyer did not hear anything. I turned to the secretary, and she had a smile on her face and said, "I'm glad someone else finally heard it too. It's the kids from the orphanage. Sometimes when we're the only people up here at night, we can hear children running down the hallway." The old lawyer dismissed the incident, while on our way out, the secretary looked at both Steve and I, and said, "I know you know what I'm talking about." We did.

If these are ghosts of children, it is a comforting thought to know they are still playing around or causing lighthearted mischief in the afterlife. But not all the entities at the Proprietary House were so much fun to deal with.

Like the spirit of Alexander, an entity called "Byron" was named such because a psychic said that was the name of one of the resident ghosts. At a time before Spirit Boxes, where we might have been able to ascertain the real name of the individual, Byron became a convenient nickname even if it was not correct. As we were deep in restoration and painting, with tools such as paint brushes routinely going missing or moving from one room to the next, we jokingly blamed him for everything. Another psychic at a separate time came in, and while not giving us a name, said there was a male ghost, African American, possibly a former slave or servant, who was not friendly. Over time, both of these became one and it was possible that Byron was an amalgamation of several entities.

To hear "slave" or "servant" was interesting. Franklin would have had several servants, Bruen owned one slave, and there is no telling if there were additional slaves owned by subsequent owners of the house, and there certainly would have been many people employed on the property over the years who could have been considered servants. Was this a real psychic connection? Did they do their homework and research the history? Or was this just the cold reading of a house, which given its age and notoriety, would have been a no-brainer to throw out there? This is why our group, while interested in what they may have to say, have shied away from using such words as evidence.

One night as we were on our way out, I was downstairs in the basement at the far end of the hallway. Steve was walking down the stairs and after a frustrating evening where he could not find one of his tools that he clearly remembered leaving somewhere in particular, he shouted up the stairs, "Thanks a lot, Byron!" As he reached the bottom step, a ladder which had been stored at the top of the stairs came crashing down behind him. I did not see the beginning of this descent, but hearing a loud banging noise, I ran towards the base of the steps to see him just get out of the way of this sliding ladder.

Did Steve anger one of the ghosts? Were they annoyed by our presence and trying to tell us to leave for the night? It would be just as easy to claim either as it would be to say that the ladder was not set down properly and the vibration of him coming down the stairs caused it to fall at a very dramatic moment. It should not have moved, given where it was, but all possible explanations needed to be explored. Nonetheless, we blamed Byron.

The stairs at the Proprietary House had long been the focal points of paranormal investigations, both by our group and visiting groups and investigators. However, aside from the incident with the ladder and one more that I still cannot explain, nothing ever happened in that area with the exception of one guest investigator capturing what sounded like a short scream on his recorder one night.

There were two separate staircases: the first led from the basement to the first floor. When you made it to the top, there was a doorway, and then a hallway. After about 10 feet, there was a second staircase that went from the first floor to the third, which was the top. The second and third floors were rented office spaces, which were locked and inaccessible, but the stairs still were accessible. Groups loved going up there with the lights out, seeing if they would experience something paranormal.

Countless minutes were spent sitting there in the dark, waiting for something to happen on the upper landings. Nothing ever had until December 21, 2011. While most of the incidents which made their way into this book and my lectures go undated, this one I remember specifically. We had a group of seven or eight people and had split up. I was with two people, Tom and Jackie Gillissie, who had come to an investigation months before and wanted to see more (they ended up becoming trustees for a brief time before a move increased their commute and made it impossible to continue volunteering), and my best friend since Kindergarten, Brett Bodner. The other group was seated in the drawing room on the first floor. We were on the top landing. The goal was to sit in silence and listen for noises. We had walkie talkies so we could communicate.

After a half hour of nothing happening, my group decided to head for the basement. We did not want to bother the other group, and figured we did not need to let them know we were moving since they would hear us coming down one flight of stairs and then the next. In the basement, we sat in the area that was called the "Tea Room" and is now the "Vault." It had no windows and was probably the darkest room in the house. Rumors persisted over the years, all stemming from visiting psychics, who claimed that the brick wall covered the entrance to a tunnel that ran from there to the bay.

They knew this because they saw a British soldier in uniform walk through the wall as if there was nothing in front of him. This legend was repeated on many tours, depending on who gave them, especially in October, though it was obviously and provably false. The basement is not entirely underground, hence why every other room down there had windows. It became so well-known that when giving a tour myself, I was asked about it by a participant before I could explain anything about the room at all.

People dreamed up all kinds of sordid things about this area of the house, given that it was the only room in the basement that looked like a basement. Although adorned with a string of lights, racks of tchotchkes that belonged in your grandmother's living room, and had tables set up for Wednesday afternoon tea services (the reason for the decor), it was a sure bet to be asked if anyone was murdered or tortured down there, and several times people remarked how it looked like a dungeon. In actuality, it was likely used by William Franklin as a wine cellar.

And so there we were, sitting, waiting. I would guess that another half hour of total silence had passed. We heard the other group get up from where they were and start to walk toward the base of the first-floor steps. We saw the light come on, as it barely emanated to where we were sitting. With that, we too got up, turned on the light, and were going to meet them. At that moment, I heard a commotion followed by a bang and a scream, and then more commotion. The four of us ran upstairs and were met by Steve and the others who all had terrified looks on their faces. Steve grabbed me and said, "How did you guys get down there?" He was totally perplexed. I informed him that we changed our minds and headed to the basement a half hour into the investigation, walked right past them, and were down there the whole time.

He was convinced this was not possible, and after a lot of back and forth (and convincing him that there was only one way down), he explained what happened. Apparently, we moved so quietly that they did not hear us. After they had turned the light on, they aimed a flashlight upstairs and were calling for us, not realizing where we were. At that moment, several of the group were looking up and saw faces and shadows staring down at them. That explained the bang, when one person jumped back and knocked something over, and another screamed out of fright. They thought it was us trying to scare them or play a joke, until those faces and shadows disappeared.

What do I make of this remarkable story, since I was present but did not see what they saw? Given how rattled everyone was, and the fact that no one was there for the first time and had spent many times at the Proprietary House in the dark, it seems certain they saw something. Shadowy figures were frequently seen, usually out of the corner of someone's eye, or darting so fast that you might not know what to make of it. But this group saw faces, and the shadow figures remained for several seconds. We soon ended the investigation because most people had enough for the night.

To me, there are two explanations if I tell myself I sincerely believe what they had to say: 1) Sometimes the light can play tricks during an investigation. Since we spend a lot of time in the dark, it takes the eyes some adjusting to get used to it. This can make it seem like something, namely a shadow figure, is moving in the dark when nothing is moving at all. Perhaps a combination of sitting in the dark for an hour, then quickly turning on a light while already hyped up from being in a haunted house caused them to see what they thought was a group of people, and, via mass hysteria, everyone managed to get freaked out and so unnerved that they needed to leave. 2) They saw exactly what they said they saw, and it was one of the best paranormal experiences one could ever hope for.

The only evidence I personally have of a shadow figure is one picture I snapped in 2011. As we often did when beginning an investigation, we would walk around the house taking pictures in every room. Some pictures contained orbs, which are highly debatable forms of evidence of spirit energy, and most images had nothing noteworthy at all. On one night, Jake had thought he saw a shadow move in the basement hallway and enter the room directly across from the vault. I went in, took a bunch of pictures, and captured nothing. But then I turned and snapped one looking out from that room, across the hall, and into the vault. A strange blob-like shadow had appeared in the photograph. It was the only picture to feature anything strange.

Maybe this was what Jake had seen. Maybe it was Byron. Maybe it was a technological fault in the camera. But one of the reasons we take so many pictures is to try to rule out if there is something wrong with the camera one is using, or if there is residual dust present causing orbs, or even if shadows, lights, and reflections combined with the flash of a camera are contributing to an anomaly that looks paranormal. I cannot prove this is a shadow figure, but it is as close as I have ever gotten to capturing one on camera.

By 2013, I was going for my history degree, coaching hockey, working as a substitute teacher, and teaching history-themed electives at a private school in Atlantic Highlands. The commute to Perth Amboy for a volunteer position was becoming too much, and with several parents encouraging me to help with that town's historical society (and to act in a "Haunted House" fundraiser), I bid farewell to the Proprietary House.

It was a difficult decision since it was so incredibly rich in history, but also because I had to leave my ghostly friends behind too. I thought back to that very first visit, and then becoming a trustee and being at meetings, hearing footsteps above where we were all sitting. At one board meeting, a door to the room we were sitting in unlatched itself, opened, and closed again. I thought about how lucky I was to be involved at such a majestic place for four years.

But there would be new adventures ahead, and many at that. I did not have to wait long, either. The historical society I would join next (I was reluctant at first—I just wanted to help out occasionally) would operate a museum that was just as, if not more, haunted than the Proprietary House, and give my team and I unmatched access to be able to investigate and collect information whenever we wanted to be used for fundraising events. These stories will be saved for the last chapters, as I feel the beginning and the end should spotlight two of my favorite places.

William Franklin as governor. (*Journal of the American Revolution/ New York Public Library*)

Benjamin Franklin with a kite and key in his famous experiment on electricity. William assists him. This is one of the only scenes most people have in mind involving Benjamin's forgotten son, memorialized by Currier and Ives for the Centennial in 1876.

This is the earliest known photograph of the Proprietary House, showing its original expansive property, taken in 1936. Houses now stand where the road is, and Kearney Avenue runs through much of the front lawn. (*Library of Congress*)

*Above:* A close-up view of the Proprietary House in 1936. (*Library of Congress*)

*Right:* A common pictorial view of the Proprietary House, which unfortunately does not convey just how large the building really is, as well as the fact that the second building hides behind it.

The back of the Proprietary House, where the 1809 addition, which would eventually serve as a hotel, orphanage, and retirement home, can be seen.

It was at this door that William Franklin was arrested in 1776, under direction from the Provincial Congress of New Jersey.

The view of the Proprietary House that would be seen by a motorist driving down Kearney Avenue. Would it be possible for ghostly figures to be viewed out of those side windows in such a scenario?

A photograph taken by the author in 2011 showing a potential shadowy figure lurking in the basement in the doorway of the vault.

**2**

# SANDY HOOK: A SPIRITED PENINSULA

## GATEWAY NATIONAL RECREATION AREA AND FORT HANCOCK HISTORIC DISTRICT, HIGHLANDS

As New Jersey's last royal governor was being chased from his comfortable home by patriots in Perth Amboy, the British Army and a band of loyalists were building a headquarters on a peninsula known as Sandy Hook for its shape. This land was strategic both locally and for the greater picture of the war. It was the gateway of Monmouth County to the British army, which as a whole would become a literal "Crossroads of the American Revolution."

From the entrance to the tip, it spans about 6 miles, but its importance is immeasurable. To the west and south are the Navesink and Shrewsbury Rivers which empty into Sandy Hook Bay. The Atlantic Ocean is to the east. Lower New York Bay is north, and Brooklyn, which contained the British stronghold in New York City, is less than 10 miles away by boat. A total 25,000 British soldiers saw themselves ferried to Sandy Hook and the surrounding areas between 1776 and 1783. It is no wonder that their army occupied this piece of land longer than any other during the American Revolution.

While encamped on Sandy Hook, the British launched hundreds of raids throughout Monmouth County. This led the colony's next governor, William Livingston, to refer to the county as the "theater of spoil and destruction." Perhaps more important than geography was the Sandy Hook Lighthouse, which had been erected near the edge of the northern point in 1764 and is currently the oldest working lighthouse in the entire United States. When the Continental Army realized they were not going to be able to hold the land, it was ordered to be destroyed or at least be rendered unusable to the British. The task was given to Major William Malcolm, with the following order:

[To] endeavor to take the glass out of the lantern and save it if possible; but if you find it impracticable, you will break the glass. You will endeavor to pump oil out of the cisterns into casks and bring it off, but if you should be obstructed in your tasks by the enemy, you will pump it to the ground. In short, you will use your best discretion to render the lighthouse entirely useless.

This occurred in March 1776, and Malcolm was successful in removing lamps and oil. However, as expected, Sandy Hook needed to be left unguarded and was subsequently captured by the British in April, who had the lighthouse operational by June. Shortly after, the Continentals attempted to attack the British-occupied light but were driven back when warships in the bay joined the battle with heavy cannon fire. The patriot force did manage to fire twenty-one cannon shots at the lighthouse, but apparently none were strong or high enough to cause serious damage, and it has remained a steady sentinel ever since. There is no record if anyone was killed in this battle.

Following the British occupation after American victory in the war, the area around the lighthouse became Fort Hancock, which housed the United States military from 1857 until 1974. It was designed by an Army Corps of Engineers captain who would rise to the rank of colonel by the start of the American Civil War, when he joined the Confederate Army. His name was Robert E. Lee.

Numerous buildings, from housing for officers and men to a church and even a theater and baseball field for recreation, were constructed over the next century. There were also no less than eighteen gun batteries, with cannon barrels ranging from 3–15 inches. At one point, the amount of guns amassed was 173. Most of these buildings still stand, though in varying degrees of decay and deterioration. Some are off-limits to visitors for this reason. One of the more popular beaches on Sandy Hook today was used as a proving ground for testing guns and their missiles, while a small structure that serves as a public restroom was once the morgue, or "Dead House" as the marker out front states.

Fort Hancock became part of the potential defense for New York City during both world wars, given its proximity, should it have been attacked by either the Japanese or Germans, and had a Nike missile defense system during the Cold War.

More than 200 years of military occupation, fighting, numerous deaths (mostly accidental or natural causes), armies coming and going, patriotism, loyalty, and swirling passions would make the Sandy Hook peninsula seem to be a prime hunting ground for paranormal activity. I have been fortunate to work there for the last eight years with a school field trip program called the Ocean Institute, which was started at Brookdale Community College and is now with Clean Ocean Action. A typical day includes seining in the bay, going over marine biology specimens, and then getting into some of the history by taking the schoolchildren to the Fort and touring some of the ruins. The question was always inevitably asked by either a student or an accompanying chaperone or teacher, "Is this place haunted?"

Being National Park Service grounds make it tricky to answer, or at least investigate for oneself. The American Littoral Society, which is housed at the Fort, usually offers ghost tours once a year in October, and that seems to be the only night when such talk is sanctioned. I have never been able to attend one of these tours since it has always occurred when hosting one of my own events.

Doing a brief search online, which is the best and worst place for looking up legends, does not churn up much, except several sources saying the ghost of famed patriot militia captain Joshua Huddy haunts the beaches of Sandy Hook. While Huddy's name would strike a chord with anyone who lives locally, he was actually killed across the river in what is now downtown Highlands. There likely would not be any reason for him to be on the Hook unless he wanted to view the site of his demise from afar.

As a worker, though, I have personally heard a couple of stories of ghostly activity told to me by someone with many more years of experience on Sandy Hook than I will likely ever accumulate. This person once spent the night in one of the abandoned officers' quarters and he and his group (they were volunteers for an organization not thrill-seekers who had broken in) heard footsteps walking on the floor above them all night.

Another story passed down to me was of an artillery soldier in the late 1800s who was accidentally killed when firing a double-barreled cannon used to destroy the masts of ships. There was a ball placed in each barrel, with a chain connecting them so as it flew towards a ship it would slice through masts and sails. Apparently only one cannon went off, the other misfiring, and the ball on one end swung around with the chain and cut the soldier in half. His spirit still remains, doomed to not move on.

There is no way to confirm if any of this is true, just as there is no way to tell how many people have died on Sandy Hook and how many of them still remain both literally and in the metaphysical realm. The more gory something is usually means less likelihood of it being real. A ghoulish tale of a soldier being cut in half sounds more like a campfire story meant to scare people under the light of a full moon than trying to find a place in the historical record. But I have heard it from two different people who are unconnected to each other and therefore need to consider it, as it is not that outlandish compared to stories associated with other locations.

The only precise area concerning death would be a simple stone monument adorned with a British flag, which may seem out of place so close to a former American military installation. It is located about 3 miles past the toll booths on the right-hand side of the road and overlooks the Horseshoe Cove section of Sandy Hook Bay from across the street. The popular bike path runs right through. This structure is known as the Halyburton Memorial.

On New Year's Eve 1783, a British ship anchored in the bay was about to return home to England. The Treaty of Paris had just been signed and the American Revolution had recently come to an end. They were having a desertion problem in their final days, and the last straw was when a group of six soldiers jumped overboard and swam to a party of patriots waiting for them nearby to escort them to safety. The ship, HMS *Assistance*, tasked Lt. Hamilton Douglas-Halyburton to chase after and capture the deserters. He took thirteen men with him and boarded a small boat. Shortly after, a fierce winter storm hit and lasted for two days. The expedition never returned, and when the snow stopped falling, their boat was found stuck in the mud, which was likely a sandbar in the Cove, and all had frozen to death. The escapees apparently made it safely away as there is no telling of what became of them, and no additional remains were ever recovered. Halyburton's mother was a dowager countess and paid to have the remains of all fourteen men buried in a mass grave with a memorial built above it.

However, in 1808, a French vessel stopped near Sandy Hook and the sailors saw a British monument and destroyed it, desecrating the grave in the process. It would go forgotten for exactly 100 years, when the U.S. Army at nearby Fort Hancock was doing construction and accidentally found the remains. There is only one photograph in existence of this event. Ironically, fourteen soldiers can be seen posing with what appears to be one skull and several leg bones sticking out of a wooden crate. Two are standing in a vault-like cave which housed the remains. If there are any pictures showing more skeletal remnants, they are not public or have been lost to time. After realizing who they belonged to and communicating with the British government, the bones were transferred to Cypress Hills Cemetery in Brooklyn where they rest today. The mass grave would go unmarked yet again until 1937, when the memorial that stands there now was constructed.

As a historian, knowing where this remarkable tragedy happened is a sobering reminder of the human element of war—of some soldiers who had enough and wanted out, and others who remained duty-bound to the very end. The paranormal investigator in me, though, was curious if this disturbed gravesite has any paranormal energy or ghostly presence. You can stand on the bayside beach overlooking the water. In the distance is the town of Highlands (most of which is quite low and at sea level). There are many waterfront restaurants today, as there have been for well over a century. In the summer, you can see hundreds of people off in the distance enjoying themselves. But you can also picture what it would have looked at in Halyburton's time.

In January 2023, my group (now Ghosts on the Coast) and I conducted a paranormal investigation at the memorial and filmed a short documentary of its history. It was the perfect time to be there, as the lack of traffic and tourists combined with frigid temperatures and hellacious wind that nearly prevented clear audio from being recorded put us right in the moment. The dark gray skies cast a gloomy glow over the bay, and you could almost see the *Assistance* docked and a small skiff getting ready to go on her mission. As we moved more inland towards the actual memorial and burial site and away from the edge of the water, the wind died down and there was an eerie silence which is what you hope for during an investigation.

In the previous nine years, almost all investigations had been at indoor locations and historic sites. But this was the year we were going to explore new and different points of interest, some of which are outside and lesser known, not just for paranormal activity but in general. Literally thousands of people pass by this monument every day in the summer, but few realize why it is there and many could not be bothered to care.

Investigating outdoors can be tricky—the natural light makes reading K-2 and EMF meters difficult, and the ambient noises around (plus not being contained within a room) make it harder to analyze EVP and SB-7 recordings.

My co-investigators for this outing, long-time friend and videographer Patrick Osborn and our group's newest member Christian Seuffert, and I did not know what to expect. For all we knew, we were the first people to investigate the spot. I thought we might find something, since disturbances of gravesites are often catalysts for hauntings. This area was desecrated once and disturbed twice. While the remains were disinterred, it stands to reason that not all of them were recovered due to the hasty nature of their removal and a less-than-forensic approach which might have left small bone fragments aplenty. Our team has always put history first, and to me, this investigation was about trying to reach into the past to talk to Revolutionary War soldiers, not born out of some morbid curiosity for shock value. The spirits ended up being quite talkative through the SB-7 radio.

I prefaced the beginning of our session with saying that it is likely no one has ever tried to communicate with any spirits at that location and instructed them that if they are present and have something to say, to speak loud and clear in the hopes that our device will catch it. Oftentimes, words or phrases come through jumbled or too quick, which Patrick spends the extra time not only analyzing the recordings but slowing it down and adding captions for viewers. In some cases, we watch the entire chunk of footage (several hours cut down into a manageable fifteen to twenty minutes) together and still cannot agree on what something says.

The first question I asked was if we could speak to Halyburton himself. The response was an immediate "Who's that?" or "Who's there?"—it was hard to make out. So, either the spirit did not know who Halyburton was (with how many people came and went on Sandy Hook in the last 200 years, it is certainly possible, especially if this spirit lived before the discovery of the mass grave) or he wanted to know who was asking. It is sometimes difficult to investigate a place for the first time, coming in with something loud and hectic like a Spirit Box and demanding answers to questions from ghosts who maybe no one ever tried to reach out to before. We are spoiled by the places we get to investigate regularly, such as the Proprietary House, and as you will see in future chapters, the Strauss Mansion in nearby Atlantic Highlands. Following that answer to my question, my SB-7 died despite having a full charge, and so we switched to our backup.

We then asked if any of Halyburton's men were there, and a female voice responded with "There's four," followed by if there are any remains left, to which we were told "his," without any additional specification. This type of chatter went back and forth for several minutes, with responses being direct but also vague. "How many men were buried here?" was met with the answer of "five." We know it was fourteen, so either the spirit had no idea and was guessing, or maybe it literally meant there were five at the exact spot we were standing at, with more elsewhere.

Of all the responses through the SB-7 while at the memorial, there was one that specifically tied us to the time period. It was a single word, "skilly," which I had to look up. As it happens, skilly was a type of gruel or porridge consisting mainly of oatmeal and was eaten regularly aboard British vessels in the eighteenth and nineteenth centuries. Surprisingly, most of the activity we captured was not by the monument but further back in the wooded area behind it. We surmised that perhaps the original location of the grave is not exactly where the current monument stands. This then led us to a small nondescript building, which was probably just an old, abandoned maintenance shed, where the voices kept coming through nonstop.

As we started to walk a small path, which eventually twisted and turned to the shed, a male voice said "walk" as if it was observing our movements. Before we could absorb that, three different voices, both male and female, came through almost simultaneously which we were not able to understand at the moment. A strong female presence then made herself known by uttering "gun," a very appropriate word, followed by, "He loved them." Was she talking about Halyburton's relationship to his soldiers? There was no way to identify this spirit, and the fact that so many female voices were heard in this spot was unusual given the military setting. But paranormal investigations always churn up such surprises, as we never know exactly who we might encounter, especially on such a storied piece of land.

Shortly after, as we neared a concrete sewage-like structure, I probed if there were any Continental soldiers perhaps lurking about, but my question of "Did you fight for George Washington?" was answered with, "Who?" We moved again on a sandy path, trying to take in the surroundings. A string of chatter was heard through the Spirit Box, sounding more like the ghosts talking to themselves instead of us. This often happens, both when using this device and recording EVPs. Investigators, including myself and my team, usually tend to assume that any response we get is directed at us when possibly we are just listening in on someone else's conversation. This explains why so many recordings do not make any sense to us as we try to decipher what they are saying. They are not saying random words to us because they might not be talking to us at all. There were well over fifty responses on this short investigation, most of which are not important enough to be reported here because they fall under that category.

We kept walking, and as Patrick pointed out two separate paths, one to the right and one to the left, a voice said "starboard." Did it want us to take the right path? Unfortunately, while we heard something in the moment, it took later analysis to understand the word. We ended up going left.

Patrick noticed the shed and found an open window to stick the camera. We turned the Spirit Box off and there was total silence. Inside, numerous animal bones were scattered throughout, and oddly enough, there was a drumstick (of the musical instrument variety, not the food) near the skull of what was probably a bird. Either someone was doing a ritual, fooling around, or another animal savagely devoured this bird due to the bones being everywhere. To my knowledge, the shed has no historical significance. As soon as we turned the Spirit Box back on, though, a woman said "hello."

There were then several other greetings, such as "hey" and another "hello." Christian asked who we were talking to, and we got our first name of the investigation: "Anna." I followed up with, "You're not from the Revolution, are you?" which garnered a "nope" and "spirit." A few minutes later, I placed a K-2 meter on the windowsill, and we heard "Stephen" and then a couple of profane expressions. It is important, and yes, mildly funny, when we get cursed at through the SB-7, because skeptics will say that words we are hearing are just from the radio, but using profanity is not allowed to be broadcast, so we know a radio station would not be such a source.

As I joked that either Patrick or Christian would be light enough to lift up through the window and into the structure, two full sentences were immediate but in varying degrees of acknowledging what I said: a lighthearted and encouraging "Okay, I'm on it," followed by a different voice saying sternly to "keep off." We had no intention of going in there anyway.

We ended the investigation with a final Spirit Box session where we started, back by the monument. This time, there was hardly any chatter at all, just the white noise coming through from the scanning of frequencies. It is ironic that both attempts by the supposed area of burial were much quieter than on the trail and near the sewer and shed.

A lot of the voices we encountered on this day were female, with few references to the time period of the American Revolution. Maybe Halyburton and his thirteen men are resting peacefully after all. Though we did receive one last message, as I thanked any spirits present for putting up with us, the words "Thanks to you" came through just before we turned off the SB-7 for the day.

I encourage people to not only check out the video footage but to stop and visit this semi-forgotten memorial and pay their respects. A note we found on the ground at the base of the monument next to a poppy flower on the day of filming read, "Dear fellow Brits: There is a corner of some foreign field that is forever England. Some of us never make it home. Love, Emily." It was nice to see that somebody cared enough for this momentary and thoughtful pause.

One might want to even try a little investigating of their own. None of the land we were on was restricted. I believe Sandy Hook to be a treasure trove of potential paranormal evidence just waiting to be tapped into. While it would be impossible to get permission to investigate inside the many buildings and former quarters in the Fort Hancock area, outside is a different story if you remain in public areas and within the operating hours of the park. It would be like investigating the Gettysburg battlefield: the park service would never condone it, but they cannot stop you either.

In addition to the former Halyburton mass grave, I have it on good authority that there is one more on Sandy Hook, though these bodies still remain. I have been sworn to secrecy, so all I can say is that it is "near the lighthouse." The exact location is known by only a select few people, and I was fortunate enough to be let in on this secret. The grave belongs to the bodies of those who perished at sea and washed up on shore and were buried by various lighthouse keepers over the years. The surrounding waters had long been seen as treacherous, which was the reason for its construction in 1764.

The New Jersey Maritime Museum Shipwreck Database lists 4,594 identified shipwrecks and ship-involved incidents or accidents off the coast of the state as a whole, with 691 having happened in the vicinity of Sandy Hook. As for unidentified, there are 680 more, with ninety-one occurring there. The oldest known catastrophe dates to December 19, 1705, when a privateer ship, the *Castle Del Rey* under the captaincy of Otto Van Tyle, encountered bad weather upon leaving New York. It ran aground on the "east bank" of the Hook, according to a newspaper report from the time. There, it weakened and gradually filled with water but did not sink right away. Rescue attempts stalled for two days due to the weather, and by the time other boats arrived with help, it was discovered that the captain and 132 of the 145 souls of English, Scottish, Irish, and Dutch descent aboard ship had already died in the frigid temperatures.

Like Halyburton's mission, most were found frozen to death still on-ship, while others drowned outright, perhaps in attempts to swim away. Of the 690 additional cataloged incidents on this list, they range from sinkings to groundings, strandings, collisions with other vessels, and all kinds of technical malfunctions—internal mechanical explosions are also incorporated. Some of these saw no death at all and were a little more than harmless, while others such as the *Castle Del Rey* experienced tremendous losses of life. Over 100 more can be tied to the waters of nearby towns such as Highlands, Atlantic Highlands, Middletown, and Navesink.

The numbers do not lie, and a good percentage of these bodies had to end up somewhere if they did not descend to the ocean floor. Even if not directly drifting to Sandy Hook, the beaches of the entire Jersey Shore are dotted with graves, most of which are long-forgotten and no longer known. I am not trying to be grim when I say that next time you are lying in the sun on your beach towel and perhaps getting ready to take a swim to cool off, you may be closer to the human remains of an old sailor or soldier than you ever figured in your wildest dreams.

As for the secrecy of this possible mass grave, it probably started to prevent relic hunters and further disturbance. It bears no marker and there is no way to know exactly how many remains may be present. The geography near the Sandy Hook Light has changed dramatically over the centuries due to littoral drift. It was once right on the water, but the ocean current has pushed the sand farther and farther—it is now more than a mile away from the tip. While I do believe the National Park Service to be unnecessarily strict on certain matters, I have respected the sentiment to keep the location safe. As tempting as it would be to conduct an investigation there, since it is not in a restricted area, there would be no way to film it without people realizing where it is.

Also located in this area was once a motley collection of shacks and tents known as "Refugeetown." While the British were building a stronghold on Sandy Hook, they were also offering protection to loyalists in the Jersey Bayshore area who may have been finding themselves under threats of violence by patriot neighbors. These loyalists were both white and black, the latter of which was predominantly made of runaway slaves who escaped to join the British Army. Following an emancipation proclamation by Virginia's Royal Governor Lord Dunmore in 1775, offering freedom to any slave who would join the British Army, thousands would attempt to leave servitude for this opportunity.

One of these slaves was a man named Titus, who became nicknamed Tye. He left his farm in Colts Neck and headed for Virginia. Some say he walked, while others allege that he made his way to a ship and sailed south. Regardless, traveling undetected after his master John Corlies had already placed a runaway slave advertisement in local papers was no small feat. In Virgina, he joined the newly formed Ethiopian Regiment, which was created by Dunmore. Tye returned to New Jersey, fighting at the Battle of Monmouth in 1778, establishing himself as a leader and given the honorary title of "Colonel."

While there are no ghost stories associated with Tye, his exploits certainly fall under the classification of "Legendary." His men were stationed at Sandy Hook, and often worked in conjunction with white British soldiers. He was eventually given his own special forces unit called the Black Brigade and used Sandy Hook and Refugeetown as a launching point for raids all over the Bayshore and Monmouth County. These actions were bold and instilled terror in the local patriot population.

More threatening to the fabric of New Jersey slaveholding society was that most of the black soldiers under Tye's command were also former slaves from the immediate area, and they specifically targeted the properties of former masters and their friends for plundering and vandalism, and also freeing additional slaves along the way. Dunmore had initially gone so far as to have the regiment's first uniforms emblazoned with the phrase "Liberty to Slaves" across the breasts of their coats. The British saw them as valuable, not only for use in guerilla warfare and boosting their own numbers, but also their knowledge of the terrain, and how they might pass through roads, forests, and rivers without being seen.

They partly rose to prominence due to the involvement of William Franklin who had returned to the fight for the British after his arrest and subsequent exile in Connecticut, though now living in New York. The Black Brigade was used in possibly hundreds of raids, large and small, from Staten Island to Sandy Hook, and a good deal farther inland. Franklin knew there was a loyalist anger that needed tapping into to combat the swelling patriotism in the area.

Tye had two interactions with famous local patriots, both ending in death. His brigade was a part of several interracial fighting forces, as the British were more colorblind than their American adversaries. Men under Tye targeted the home of Joseph Murray in Middletown, which is now part of the Poricy Park Nature Conserve. Murray was a member of the local militia and had personally been involved in the execution of loyalists and his name made its way to the British. The final straw was the alleged theft of a horse from the home of influential loyalist Edward Taylor, which still stands as Marlpit Hall, about 3 miles away.

One afternoon as Murray was plowing his field, three men emerged from the woods bordering the farm and shot him in the back. As he lay dying, they approached and finished him off with bayonets. Tye himself was not present. A monument near the site of this execution reads, "On June 8, 1780 at this site, Joseph Murray was murdered by Tories in retaliation for his daring patriot deeds." To the British, those deeds would have been seen as murder and theft.

Retaliation was a common word in the Bayshore area. The patriots had their own militia unit called the "Monmouth Retaliators," which was everything it sounded like. Joshua Huddy was a member, and after years of executing loyalists and evading capture by the British, his luck temporarily ran out against Tye. A little more than two months after leaving Murray's body bloody in his field, Tye and a mixed-race force, which included the prominent Queen's Rangers commanded by the infamous John Graves Simcoe, surrounded Huddy's house in Colts Neck and laid siege. Huddy fended them off for several hours with the assistance of his mistress Lucretia Emmons who had several pre-loaded muskets at the ready near windows. He fired while she reloaded. Huddy only surrendered after the house was set ablaze.

Tye had captured the most valuable villain the patriots had to offer. But Huddy's luck returned as he was being escorted by rowboat to Sandy Hook for likely disposition to prison in New York and eventual trial and execution, and he was spotted by patriots on the shore. They opened fire on the boat and Huddy managed to swim away. Tye was shot in the wrist and died two weeks later from a combination of tetanus, lockjaw, and infection. There is no record of where he lived out his remaining days nor where he was buried. Would it be a stretch to say also on Sandy Hook?

Huddy, meanwhile, lived another two years before being captured once and for all in 1782 in Toms River and brought back to Highlands. It was there, in the park that bears his name, that he was hanged by the neck until dead in retaliation for his execution of British soldier Philip White. A note pinned to the chest of his swinging corpse defined that as the reason. All of this happening across the river from Sandy Hook and just a couple of miles away from where Tye met his end.

All told, over 1,000 residents of Monmouth County suffered from violence in some way during the American Revolution. Between being killed in battle, executed, wounded, imprisoned, vandalized, robbed, or tormented by people in opposition, how many souls still linger, unable to move on? So many lives snuffed out, so much unfinished business, which is usually associated with being one of the causes for hauntings. It would be impossible to investigate every site known to have activity, and a lot of the locations are either gone physically or simply lost to time.

There are signs and markers all over the Bayshore area telling of a British campsite or that their army passed by a certain point. Sandy Hook boasts several as well but does not tell the complete story. Whether you are only interested in history or truly believe in ghosts, walking by the lighthouse and some of the other buildings near dusk (especially in the fall) can be a truly magical experience. You can picture the soldiers and the great warships out in the bay, and maybe hear the cannons roar. Perhaps you will see Colonel Tye and his brigade who have ultimately been written out of history, like William Franklin, for not being on the right side at the war's conclusion. The story of their existence would have been history-altering otherwise.

As you make your drive home from Sandy Hook and near the bridge that crosses the Shrewsbury River, it is impossible to not notice the massive Navesink Twin Lights Lighthouse looming on the hillside overlooking the peninsula and Atlantic Ocean. Some days when we had school trips for the Ocean Institute and it was raining, we would bring the buses up there to get the kids out of the rain and do our programs inside. The day would be completed with a tour of the building and bringing groups up to one of the lights so they could see the incredible views.

People always ask if Twin Lights is haunted, and honestly, I could not tell you. While ghost stories from various sources both official and unofficial have escaped Sandy Hook and Fort Hancock, there are none, to my knowledge, from Twin Lights which is state-owned. In fact, one day when we had a group up there and I was speaking to the caretaker at the time, I politely asked them if there were any ghost stories associated with the lighthouse. The individual proceeded to give me one of the most magnificently sneering eyerolls I had ever seen and walked away. They never spoke to me again any other time I was up there for a trip.

The structure dates to 1862, built during the American Civil War. It served as an important beacon to ships coming and going from New York City in addition to the Sandy Hook Lighthouse built nearly 100 years earlier. The number of shipwrecks already discussed made these additional lights necessary. One of the lights was solid, while the other blinked, allowing it to be identified by captains from afar. There was a previous lighthouse at the site dating nearly forty years earlier, but it was not effective enough.

Various other notable achievements at the property span both science and culture: it was the first lighthouse to use a Fresnel Lens, which allowed the greater magnification and projection of a smaller light source to be used as the illuminating element, the Marconi Company tested a wireless telegraph at the site in 1899, and in 1893, the Pledge of Allegiance was recited publicly there for the first time.

While a site like the Proprietary House which is also state-owned has tolerated (and in some cases encouraged) ghost tours and paranormal programming over the years as a means of fundraising income, it appears that desire does not exist at Twin Lights. It is understandable that they wish to remain strictly a historic site and do not want to be known for anything ghoulish. However, if they read this book and happen to change their mind, I would love to be the first to investigate.

*Left:* The Sandy Hook Lighthouse at dusk. It has been lit, with few interruptions, since 1764 and is the nation's oldest operating lighthouse.

*Below:* The former morgue at Fort Hancock. It is now a public restroom.

*Above:* The only known likeness of the HMS *Assistance* in existence. This sketch was done thirteen years after the Halyburton tragedy in 1796. The ship lasted only six more years before being wrecked in 1802.

*Right:* The Halyburton Memorial, captured on an overcast January afternoon.

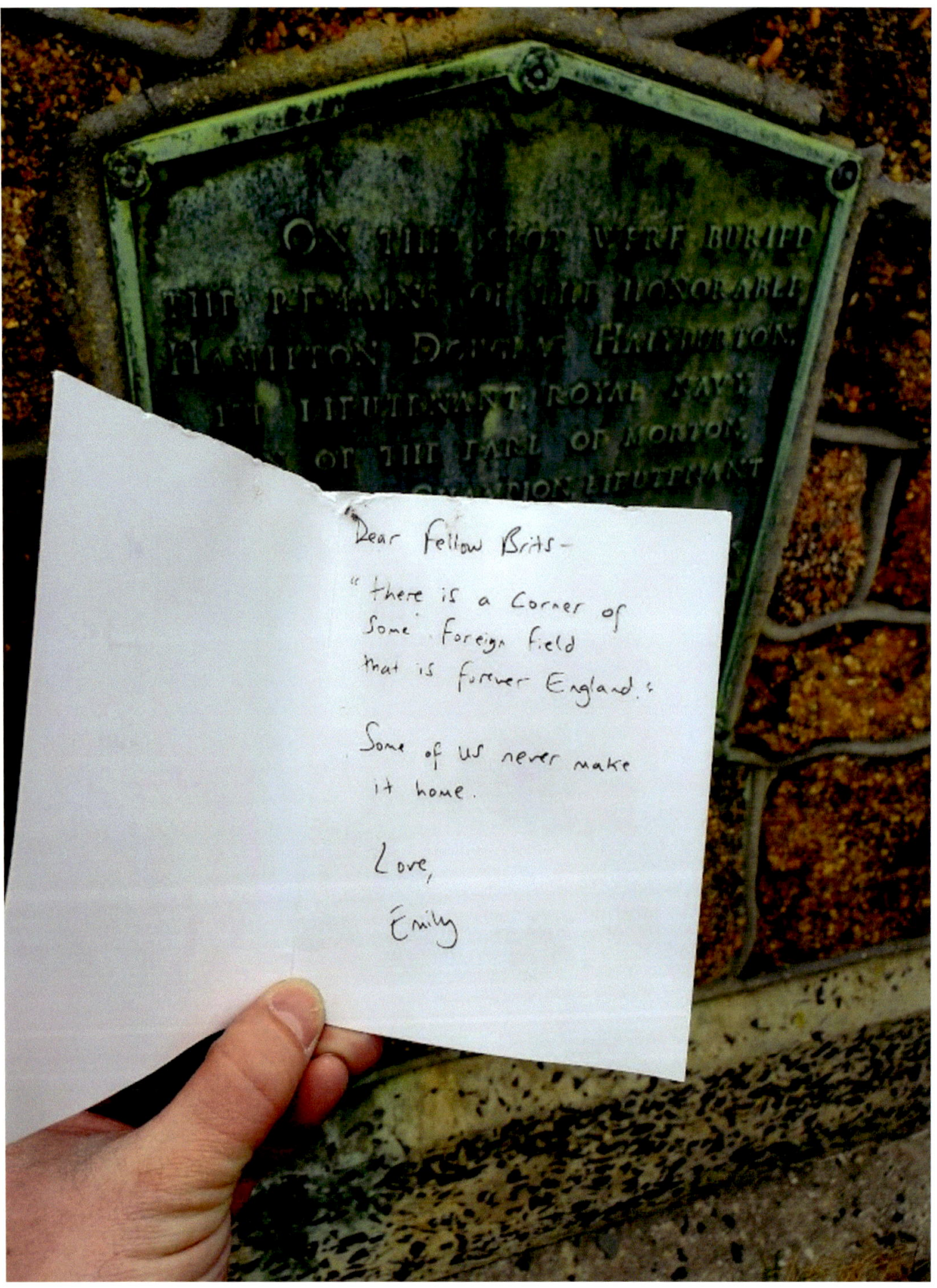


The note left by a visitor to the Halyburton Memorial that was found by the Ghosts on the Coast crew prior to filming.

It was a muddy area like this where Halyburton's boat became trapped in a winter storm, causing them to freeze to death. (*Ghosts on the Coast/ Patrick Osborn*)

A remarkable photograph of the 1908 discovery of the remains of Halyburton and his men. This is the only one known to exist. (*Nauvoo to the Hook/ Henry Sandlass*)

A 1790 drawing of what the original monument to Halyburton looked like prior to being destroyed in 1808. (*Nauvoo to the Hook/ New York Magazine*)

Greg and Christian peer into the abandoned maintenance shed during their investigation of the area surrounding the Halyburton memorial. (*Ghosts on the Coast/Patrick Osborn*)

Christian holds the SB-7 a few feet behind the Halyburton memorial. (*Ghosts on the Coast/ Patrick Osborn*)

Animal bones scattered around the floor of the abandoned shed. (*Ghosts on the Coast/ Patrick Osborn*)

# 3

# THE CURSE OF HUDSON SPRINGS?

## HENRY HUDSON SPRINGS AND HENRY HUDSON TRAIL, ATLANTIC HIGHLANDS

A few miles away from where Joshua Huddy escaped Colonel Tye and made it safely to shore, 171 years earlier, there was a landing of a different kind about to occur. In 1609, explorer Henry Hudson was sailing up the coast of New Jersey aboard his ship the *Halve Maen* (anglicized as *Half Moon*). He stepped foot on Atlantic Highlands soil on September 3. While in search of fresh water and game, Hudson and his men first met with the native Lenape people along the shoreline between what is now named Popamora Point in Highlands and where the Atlantic Highlands Marina currently is. It is a coast connected by a popular biking and walking path called the Henry Hudson Trail, which was also used as a rail line for the Central Railroad of New Jersey in the late nineteenth and early twentieth centuries.

Though interactions started out friendly between Hudson's men and the natives, they were warned not to do two things: drink from a freshwater spring that they had discovered, which was considered to have magical properties, or disturb the sacred land around it. While his superstitious crew seemed eager to listen, Hudson did not. What happened next was a chain of unfortunate events that may have led to the captain's untimely demise less than two years later, or so the legend or "curse" has it. In search of new content in 2023, I stumbled upon this story by accident via a little known re-published *Weird N.J.* article from 2017. While some legends published by the popular magazine take off and become popular and unrelenting points of interest with visitors, this one has seemingly remained relatively unknown.

The spring itself, the facade of which has been altered over time, is known only hyper-locally, and the curse was apparently so far-fetched that when posting our documentary titled *The Curse of Hudson Springs* to local Facebook groups, we were met with equal parts backlash as curiosity, as lifelong locals who grew up drinking the water as children made sure to let us know that they were perfectly fine. However, it was worth looking into, and there really was a litany of tragedies and mishaps which befell Hudson in ensuing years, which is why we went with the title we did, as well as for this book, though I have since added a question mark to the end of it for reasons about to be explained.

Then there are, of course, the legends which have persisted over the years of people seeing the spirit of Captain Henry Hudson and his ship the *Half Moon* trapped and doomed in the waters off Sandy Hook, which is visible from the spring. People just love ghost ships and tragedies at sea. But Hudson died in northern Canada and the ship he was using for that particular expedition was not the *Half Moon*, which survived Hudson by seven years before sinking in the East Indies in 1618. Be that as it may, if Hudson's men and perhaps possibly he himself believed they were cursed due to something that happened in the tranquil New Jersey Bayshore, then cursed they were.

Before exploring the river that now bears his name, Henry Hudson and his crew on the *Half Moon* arrived in the waters of Sandy Hook Bay on September 2, 1609 and observed the hills of the Navesink Highlands. The Indians on the shore watched the ship enter the waters and wondered what it could have been, possibly one of their demon gods "Manito" who was visiting them from beyond the horizon. This suggestion is put forth in Thomas Henry Leonard's 1923 authoritative history of the Atlantic Highlands area, *From Indian Trail to Electric Rail*, though, as expected for the time, he nonchalantly refers to them as "savages" every chance he had. There is no way to tell what the natives were thinking, but we know what Hudson's men were due to the logbook kept aboard ship by his first mate, Robert Juet. Ironically, these writings from more than 300 years prior to Leonard's work contain no such slurs, at least in the section pertaining to these initial interactions that I have read.

The next day, Hudson and his men came ashore in what is now Atlantic Highlands. Some went fishing and others hunted, but the search for fresh water was the more important task. They soon were greeted by the Lenni Lenape, who were described as magnificent and dressed in elk skins. Their earliest interactions were amicable, as both sides traded goods, and Hudson was gifted green tobacco. Some natives were invited aboard the *Half Moon* where the additional trading of maize occurred.

There is no mention of the spring in Juet's log at all, which is a terrible inconvenience not only to investigating the legend of a curse, but establishing its authenticity as a historic site. We have a decent timeline of what occurred at the spring from the 1800s until today, but before that is murky. It begs the question: did Hudson and his men really drink there at all? Is that a legend in itself?

But in keeping with the story, as Hudson's crewmen neared the site of the spring, they were warned that the water itself was for healing and the land was sacred, possibly a burial ground by modern analysis, and to not proceed. How this warning took place with each side not able to speak the other's language is never explained. Maybe it occurred through gesturing. The crew supposedly heeded the warning, but Hudson forced them toward the spring to collect water anyway since they had been at sea for five weeks and had nearly run out. In so doing, the land was trampled upon and desecrated.

They would make it safely back to the *Half Moon* later that day, but their journey which had been relatively tame would begin to go awry. Several men became mysteriously sick, and three days later, on September 6, a small crew on an exploratory mission in the bay was suddenly attacked by the Lenape who rowed up alongside them in a canoe. Two men were wounded, and another, John Colman, was killed—shot through the throat by a stone-tipped arrow. He is the first recorded European to be killed by a native in

New Jersey history. It took until the next day for his body to be recovered, and sources indicate he was buried in one of several places, two of them being in the Bayshore area: Point Comfort in Keansburg (where Hudson also sailed past, and according to some sources, made landfall) or what was then the tip of Sandy Hook, which Hudson named "Colman's Point" in his honor. Other sources say the killing occurred closer to where New York City is, and he is buried there.

Colman's death may be the most interesting part of this entire debacle, as the man is associated with his own ghost story, and we know for a fact he did indeed exist and was murdered. Recently, there has been a push among historians in Keansburg to have a marker placed laying claim to his place of burial happening in their town. One even says his body is buried very specifically at the end of Carr Avenue and is certain that Colman's Point became Point Comfort over time. Leonard's book, though centered around Atlantic Highlands, suggests a Keansburg burial, though a source from 1867 says he was buried on one of the beaches at Sandy Hook.

While the log gives several geographic descriptions of when the *Half Moon* was anchored off Atlantic Highlands (noting the "tall hills" and "tall oaks" of Navesink), there is nothing said about Colman's final resting place other than that he was given one. Had he been killed while rowing past Sandy Hook and his body needed to be recovered, it is likely he was buried there. There is an obscure painting of this attack on the wall of Jersey City's Hudson County Courthouse, which is of little help to anyone.

In 2009, the *New York Times* argued Colman's death is "New York's Coldest Case," not New Jersey's, and some feel he was buried at Coney Island. There can be no set reason for his murder either, as hypotheses offered have ranged from encountering unfriendly Indians unaware of Hudson's arrival in a different area to wandering too close to sacred land or the place that wampum was made, which would have been important to be kept secret. He was therefore killed to prevent word of its discovery— an explanation as good as any.

His body was put to rest somewhere, but according to Dutch folklore, his soul was not so at-ease. Following his death, he transformed into a *Dwerg*, which is a dwarf-like creature or goblin said to haunt the deepest parts of the Hudson River, near West Point, and cause the disappearance of ships over the centuries. Apparently so well known, Colman's *Dwerg* was written about by Washington Irving. This only deepens the mystery, as why would Colman's eternal spirit haunt the West Point section of the Hudson River if he was killed between Sandy Hook and New York City, and buried somewhere near there?

As for Hudson, he remained in the area until September 9, having two more incidents with the Lenape: another round of friendly trading at sea and then one final attempted attack a day later when the *Half Moon* escaped for the New York area under a hail of arrows. While his exploration of the river, which would bear his name, was a cartographic success, he did not find the elusive Northwest Passage, the goal of the expedition.

Hudson's trip was also soon plagued by peculiarities. The ship encountered problems with its masts, rigging, moorings, and sails, which inexplicably tore. Any ship on a voyage can encounter such annoyances, but the legend has each passing incident causing the crew to think back to that day at the spring where they were forced by their captain to drink the water. The relationship between Hudson and these men apparently never recovered. Less than two years later, on a separate expedition (with not all of them the same sailors, mind you) in Canada, Hudson's crew mutinied and set him and several others adrift. They were never seen again and were presumed dead shortly after.

But did any possible curse come to an end with their demise? It would seem so. In the centuries to follow, many continued to drink from the spring without issue. In the 1830s, a local merchant named Louis Despreaux pumped water from the spring down to the bay and charged 5 cents per barrel to visiting ships. Towards the latter part of the nineteenth century, the site became a tourist attraction, and the Works Progress Administration (WPA) erected a peanut stone wall, a small bridge across a gully towards the spring, pipes so that the water would be more accessible, and a base for it to collect and drain, in the 1930s.

Previously in 1891, the town of Atlantic Highlands considered building a statue of Hudson on what is now Mount Mitchill Scenic Overlook, the highest point on the eastern seaboard. This project never came to fruition, and the spring and Hudson's local notoriety became somewhat forgotten until 1977, when the Atlantic Highlands Historical Society (AHHS) cleaned up the area and placed a small plaque. But in recent years, the spring has been largely neglected again and is overgrown with weeds most of the year. It is the perfect place to visit for those who seek out the abandoned. The water that still flows is no longer safe for human consumption.

I know many people, both firsthand and through the release of our short documentary, who drank this water as children and found the idea of a curse to be asinine. It was after it already came out that I was in the office of the AHHS (where I have volunteered for nearly a decade since leaving the Proprietary House) and found an old folder that contained files on Hudson Springs, with nothing newer than 1980 inside it. "This would have been helpful last month," I thought to myself.

It was time to conduct a historical investigation, seeing if there was any mention of a curse and on top of that, if there was any evidence presented that could tie Hudson to the spring at all. What I found was a single page history of the spring from October 30, 1977 stapled to what appeared to be minutes for a monthly meeting. There was no reference to a curse or anything spooky, and as for Hudson and his men drinking that water, it was noted as "unconfirmed tradition." The only specifics into who used the spring were that it "quenched the thirst of the peaceful Lenape, replaced the rancid water on ships of early European explorers, served the armies on both sides during the Revolutionary and 1812 Wars, and was used by fishing fleets sometimes numbering 300 schooners." Who the "European explorers" were is not elaborated on, but it would have been the perfect chance to say Henry Hudson.

Nevertheless, we conducted a paranormal investigation near the spring in February 2023 which became a part of the documentary. While no one had ever claimed the site of the spring to be haunted, we wanted to investigate anyway because of the historic ties and to see if any presence remains. We got quite a bit of evidence and intelligent responses through our Spirit Box radio.

Like the Halyburton Memorial, we were likely the first people to ever attempt an investigation and were curious to see if we could uncover anything. A few moments after we started the SB-7 and I gave the spirits instructions on how to communicate with us, two voices were heard: "its him" from a male and "lost" from a female. Judging by the tone, I do not think they were speaking to us. When I asked if any of Henry Hudson's men were with us, the response was "were." I was hoping they would elaborate, but it never came. There was just another voice saying "no."

My next question was if it was safe to drink the water from the spring, and a voice clearly said "eat." Do ghosts get hungry on the other side? We turned the direction of the conversation towards the Lenape, owing to the fact that they might not understand our English and be able to respond. Christian and I both happened to ask a question at the same time, me with "Are there any Lenape here?" and him saying "Is this sacred land?" The answer was a simple "sacred." Our first name of the investigation was "Smith," which was irrelevant to the question I was asking at the time.

There were many irrelevant answers during this investigation, many of them just one word. It was frustrating, but also expected. We moved a little bit closer to the shoreline and away from the spring. I was talking to the camera at this point, saying how Hudson's men likely explored all over the area, but I did not know what would be a good place to investigate. As I finished speaking, a voice said, "This is it". We thought we reached the right spot, but when I followed up with, "Is this where you want us to stand?" we were told "no." We then heard two words that were relevant to the seafaring time period of Hudson, but not what we were directly asking about: "surf" and "harpoon." If the spirits were trying to tell us something, we were only getting it in fragments.

We headed back up to the spring itself and placed the SB-7 just feet from the actual dripping water. There were scattered responses, and as Christian changed position, Patrick filmed him almost tripping. We both joked about it, to which we heard "ha" through the device. Shortly after that was "good place." Numerous questions regarding John Colman were met with silence, except one where we heard "bled" when I asked how he died. The name "Smith" was spoken a second time, and a third a few minutes later. Who was this, and why was his name being repeated over and over again? The other word spoken three times during the investigation was "sleep."

Questions turned to the actual water itself, and a male spirit answered in the affirmative when I asked if they still drink the water in death. A Mel-Meter and K-2 scan of the spring did not turn up any exceptional spikes, but as Patrick grabbed the Mel-Meter from where it was sitting and started to hold it near the running water, we heard "Pat … wait."

Given the number of responses, we can say that there is definitely a presence of some kind at Hudson Springs, but I would not consider it haunted in the literal sense. The next question that must be posed, in thinking back to the original tale, is what made this particular piece of land sacred and was it a burial ground? The area where the bridge was contains a drop of about 20 feet. To the left of that is a modern drainage pipe and ditch that empties into a small marsh-like setting that eventually makes its way to the bay, past the Henry Hudson Trail, only 100 or so feet away.

There has been enough digging, both to install the pipeline and also in the surrounding properties where modern houses currently stand (someone's backyard is right behind the wall and entrance staircase erected by the WPA), that if there were numerous bodies scattered around, they likely would have been found. Also, with the trail having been excavated for its own installation and its former use as a train line, it pretty much rules out that possibility. But as established in the last chapter, with the resting places for bodies from hundreds of years ago (including citizen, soldier, and native) being possibly anywhere along the Bayshore, that does not mean no one is buried near the vicinity of the spring. It is likely that the label of sacred ground was added to the story at a later time to add to the mystique. As for the origin of this tale, there does not appear to be anything online or in print anywhere except that *Weird N.J.* article. I do not believe the story was created just for that, as it speaks to it already having been established. But no sources are given and no locals seem to remember ever hearing anything about spooky, except the occasional reference to Hudson's ghost sailing the bay, which sounds like it was passed down to someone regaled by an old salt.

More importantly than any of our paranormal findings, though, was the drumming up of interest in this neglected site. We unintentionally created a conversation online concerning why the area of Hudson Springs is in such bad shape. We received a lot of comments on our video on the various Facebook pages we shared it to. Most were overwhelmingly positive, save for those who wanted nothing to do with this alleged curse.

But we have to remember that a curse is only as strong as the belief in it. If Hudson's men truly believed it was cursed, then it was. Mind over matter is very much evident in paranormal investigating and folklore studies today, and this with a world of psychological and/or debunking information at our fingertips. You can imagine being a sailor in the 1600s in a strange land, thousands of miles away from home and encountering such bad luck. This was a mindset that they never quite got over according to the legend, even without a traceable origin.

The water today will not cause some superstorm of otherworldly activity for you, though it has been condemned by the town as not safe for drinking. The drinkability of the water, though, is far from central to this story. One comment that still stands out to me was something to the effect of, "The only scary thing about Hudson Springs is its neglect."

The back-and-forth history of what to do with it is almost as interesting as Hudson's potential involvement itself. After the WPA turned it into a park-like setting and added the now-collapsed and removed bridge, it fell into near-ruin and was forgotten except by locals (and most people in town today have no idea it exists). Also in the archives of the AHHS was information detailing the struggle to restore the spring in the 1970s. There were newspaper articles and architectural blueprints illustrating a proposed major restoration of the site in 1975 which never came to fruition due to lack of funding. What else is new?

While the AHHS did clean up the area and place a plaque in 1977, a full overhaul was never completed. There was an attempt again in 1980, based on a letter that was found stating that the organization would contribute $500 to repairing and maintaining the grounds if the borough of Atlantic Highlands would take on the project. However, it was assessed that necessary repairs bringing it back to former glory and fixing land erosion concerns would cost $55,000 and the town refused to consider it.

A 1975 article in the *Daily Register* blasted the town for neglect, saying, "Shame on the residents of Atlantic Highlands … to call the Hudson Springs area a disaster is inadequate…. Very few towns have been blessed with such a landmark and I pray that few towns have failed as miserably as Atlantic Highlands in their preservation." While a fundraising drive aiming for $12,000 was begun shortly after (another estimate for fixing it came in much lower), that too apparently failed.

Perhaps Hudson Springs really is cursed, but not in a supernatural sense. It may be doomed to remain overgrown and neglected for eternity as the money is not, nor ever was, there to turn it into a true historic site. Then again, we do not know if it truly is historic since Hudson cannot be pinpointed there. But its use by the Lenape could make it a site which is culturally relevant to the history of the Bayshore at large.

Just how important is it overall? It does not quite have the national appeal as, say, Plymouth Rock does, but although Henry Hudson did not literally make his first steps on New Jersey soil there, it is the first place that became associated with him and European explorers in general in New Jersey. There should be a sign saying what and where it is, at the very least. There is currently none. While one major argument against restoring the area forty years ago was that there was no place to put a parking lot for visitors, the site is accessible from the Henry Hudson Trail, which is frequented by hundreds of walkers and bikers per day. They travel right past the entrance without knowing it is there.

In a perfect world, Hudson Springs would look as it did in the postcard nearly a century ago, with the bridge and pool intact. There would be someone to maintain the area by keeping the grass and weeds in check (come summertime, the peanut stone wall is nearly entirely covered by greenery). There would be a historic marker and maybe some illustrated panels educating people on Hudson's voyage and the history of the Lenape people and their use of the site.

Whether it is cursed or haunted or nothing at all, I did feel we accomplished something due to the hundreds of comments that poured in after the documentary. This chapter also gave me the opportunity to elaborate more on its history, which was locked away in a museum archive for nearly fifty years.

When we concluded our investigation, we burned sage and spoke to the land as if the Lenape were still present, thanking them for allowing us to be there without harm, and also wishing them peace in their afterlife and hoping we did not disturb them. In actuality, it really is a peaceful, beautiful spot which could be so much more. The elevation gives a perfect view to Sandy Hook, and if the Lenape were standing there on that fateful day in September 1609, they had their first chance to see the foreign *Half Moon* arrive in their waters in a moment that certainly changed the history of the Bayshore and Greater New York City area forever.

The arrival of Henry Hudson to the waters of the Bayshore depicted in this lithograph by Frederic Chapman. Could that be Sandy Hook in the background? (*Library of Congress*)

An engraving of the Half Moon as it would have been seen during Hudson's exploration of the New York/New Jersey area in 1609. This exact spot depicted is unknown, but natives in canoes rowing up to the ship would have been a familiar sight to early Europeans in the Bayshore. (*Library of Congress*)

Hudson and his men were eventually set adrift after a mutiny in 1611. Was the crew's anger and loss of faith in their captain stemming from drinking the cursed waters of the spring? (*Library of Congress*)

*Opposite above:* Hudson Springs is depicted in a colorized postcard some time after the Works Progress Administration restored the site. (*Atlantic Highlands Historical Society*)

*Opposite below:* Details of a proposed major restoration in 1975 that were never realized. It would have added a new bridge, steps, paths, basin, and storm drain. (*Atlantic Highlands Historical Society*)

NEW FOOT BRIDGE.
LOCATION OF 48" STORM DRAIN
RIP RAP SWALE
RAILROAD TIE STEPS
TAN BARK FOOT TRAIL
COOKE & DAHER LANDSCAPE ARCHITE

The water still drips out of the spouts today, though it is no longer safe for drinking. (*Ghosts on the Coast/Patrick Osborn*)

*Opposite:* While the spring and wall can be easily seen and accessed in fall and winter, by summer it becomes so overgrown with foliage that it is nearly impossible to explore.

Videographer Patrick Osborn stands on the decaying structure to get the perfect shot. Such a drop and deterioration has long been a deterrent to restoration.

# 4

# SPY HOUSE SECRETS REVEALED

## SEABROOK-WILSON HOUSE AND BAYSHORE WATERFRONT PARK, PORT MONMOUTH

Oh, the stories I heard about the Spy House over the years. It is located only ten minutes from where I lived, but I had never visited until I met Jeff Huber. It was a brisk May evening in 2010 that he and I went for a walk on the property after the sun had set. The wind was whipping. The house is just mere feet from the bay and bordering Monmouth Cove Marina. I cannot remember if he had ever been there before, but he called me out of the blue that night saying he was in the area and asked, "Hey do you want to check out the Spy House?" Not knowing what to expect, I enthusiastically met him there. The building was closed, not just for the night, but it was nearing the end of a years-long transition period from its former stewardship under Middletown Township to its new and present owners, the Monmouth County Park System (MCPS), and then was heavily renovated.

For many years in the past and now presently, this building has managed to retain the title of either or both "Most Haunted House in New Jersey" and "Most Haunted House in America." It is the subject of profiles and features every October in some of the local newspapers and magazines. And there we were, checking it out, sticking flashlights up to the windows like so many others do on a nightly basis, and standing from afar attempting to see if we could see anything moving around. The Spy House was entirely empty due to the aforementioned transition. There was no furniture or artifacts inside, which made it easier when trying to look for any paranormal activity, because there were no physical objects that could be confused or cause a shadow or reflection back when taking a picture.

I did not have much background information at the time, save for what I read online or had heard from growing up in the area. Numerous stories of the ghosts of Revolutionary War soldiers, pirates, Lenape Indians, and, of course, spies. Many well-known psychics had seized the opportunity under past ownership to use the location as a chance to tell all kinds of wild tales. Then there was the former curator, Gertrude Neidlinger, who so many had stories about, but had since passed away.

Depending on who you asked, she was described with reverence and awe as a kind and knowledgeable soul dedicated to her own entertaining brand of historical interpretation, and also as a "crazy old lady" and a charlatan. She was a character, I was told, who could keep you on the edge of your seat with her storytelling abilities while giving tours of the house which she said dated to the mid-1600s and contained all kinds of antiques.

Never did I ever feel as amped up to be at a haunted location at this point in my life, more so than the Proprietary House on that first visit that occurred a year before this was taking place. And we were not even going inside. I documented this first visit in a blog post which is still available for viewing today. As I read it to prepare for this chapter, I laughed at several parts. The story of my investigating and researching the Spy House is one of evolution, and personal growth from an easily excitable investigator to one who has become very much a skeptic and debunker, including many moments I have witnessed myself.

Jeff and I were there for twenty minutes on this particular night. We went right up to the house, taking hundreds of pictures of probably every inch, so we could go back and look at the photos later on, seeing if we captured anything. On three separate occasions, Jeff thought he saw a shadowy figure moving in one of the upstairs windows. I believed him then, and now as well in hindsight, since by my recollection, Jeff was not prone to seeing spirits and never once saw anything in his more than a decade of service at the Proprietary House—four of those years with me. I consider myself unflappable now, but I was not back in 2010. Jeff was. Still, he and I happened to look at each other at one point and think there was some kind of negative energy present that did not want us lurking around trying to find it. I used the phrase "evil" in that initial blog post, something I do not think I would ever say today.

In our many photos that night, only one contained an anomaly (there were numerous orbs in the pictures, but I have never considered them to be hard evidence), which I spotted when I got home. In one shot of the back of the house, in a window on the first floor, there was something that looked like a figure of some sort—like a head peering out of the darkness. Maybe it is the figure Jeff saw. Future photos of that same window did not replicate the result, meaning that it is not a constant object if not paranormal.

Two months later, I returned again, this time with Brett. We parked across the street and walked to the front lawn area where there was a short white picket fence. Out of nowhere, and startling us, was a woman asking cheerfully, "Looking for ghosts?" We turned and said that we were. Her husband ended up coming over and joining us. They told us they were the owners of Jersey Joe's, a well-known Italian Hot Dog eatery located across the street which is now closed. For about a half hour, they enthralled us with stories. This is one of those encounters that just materializes from nowhere and ends up being so valuable.

They echoed a lot of the popular stories, and also told us of something called "Abigail's Window," which is located upstairs on the side facing the water. Legend had it that a woman named Abigail remains forever doomed to stare out the window as she waits for her husband who was lost at sea. There were also stories of ghost children who liked to run around on the lawn at night—they had personally seen them and heard their giggling. She also happened to tell us of a woman who came into their restaurant earlier in the day with a piece of technology that she could only describe as a "Ghost Box," which let out this loud, static sound in which they heard voices. This would have been one of the earlier versions of the device that would become the SB-7 Spirit Box.

In the next year or so, the Spy House eventually opened as the Bayshore Waterfront Park Activity Center, and it is also referred to as the Seabrook-Wilson House, in reference to two previous owners. But it is never called the Spy House by its new owners. This came after nearly twelve years of closure, as the transfer began in 1997, construction took place from 2008–2009 (partly due to a nearly $575,000 historic trust grant awarded in 2002), and then it was finally ready by late 2010. When it reopened after such heavy restoration, most locals felt the original creepy charm was ruined. I concur with that assessment.

Around this time, I had begun my lecturing career on various subjects, both historical and on the paranormal, for different organizations. In the next few years, I would become an instructor for the Lifelong Learning program at Brookdale Community College. But no matter where I was, the Spy House always came up. All I had to say, though, was what I read online and my first experiences, which really were not much despite my fear at the time.

The house finally opened, and the history provided by the MCPS seemed very sanitized. There was no mention or acknowledgment of ghosts, which is not abnormal for a historic site, but nothing about spies or pirates, which are indelible to it, either. This angered me, because it seemed like a cover-up, and I was eager to prove the dark history to be true. It did not take very long for me to realize why there was such ignorance on behalf of Monmouth County and why there was so much silence for over a decade: it was not ignorance at all, it was damage control.

While I truly believe the Spy House is haunted, I ended up uncovering many of the legends associated with the property to be untrue, and crazily so. When I debunk these, people generally see it as an attack and an overtly devious attempt to ruin the house's nationwide renown. But that is not true, because I can still believe in a haunting without giving in to what is essentially a false history created by its former caretaker. And there are various points of view on her as well.

I was also working part-time for the MCPS as a summer camp counselor and hockey coach at Dorbrook Park in Colts Neck, right down the street from where Joshua Huddy fended off Colonel Tye, and from where Laird's distillery produced liquor and spirits enjoyed by George Washington. My supervisor knew I did history talks and asked if I would do some for them. I agreed and developed a series on battles of the American Civil War which lasted for a couple of years and occurred mainly at Thompson Park in Lincroft.

In January 2011, I presented one on the American Revolution in Monmouth County, and they let me give it at the Spy House, which was my first time inside. It had recently opened to the public (come to think of it, that might have been one of the first actual events they scheduled) and was far from the creepy image I had in my mind due to the recent renovations. Only one area of the house, the older section, was left resembling its original form. I was excited to be there but was also left wondering what the rest looked like originally. The father of a well-known television paranormal investigator, who I met at the Proprietary House, attended just because he wanted to be able to sit inside. It was that big of a deal.

After lecturing on and off for the MCPS for a couple of years, the time came to plan for the fall of 2013, and I suggested a "haunted history" talk which would cover historic sites my friends and I had investigated. My boss loved the idea, and after going back and forth on the specifics, he said, "What if I could get you into the Spy House for this talk?" I was stunned, thinking how incredible that would be but also feeling that it would never happen. He proposed the idea to his superiors, and we were given shocking approval for me to conduct a lecture on the paranormal at the Spy House, but with one caveat—I could not discuss anything about the Spy House itself. It was also pushed back on the calendar and happened in February 2014.

Hearing that was a disappointment, but I was not going to pass up any opportunity to get inside. We assumed the event would sell out, and it did. We packed over thirty people into a small room for the presentation. I remember asking my boss, "What happens if someone asks if this place is haunted? You know people are going to." He responded saying that we could not control audience questions, and that it would be rude to not answer them, with a wink. Sure enough, I made my way through the talk, and at the end, numerous hands went up wanting to know more about the house we were sitting in. I told what I knew, but I think I ended up learning more than my audience on that day.

A few locals in attendance shared stories about being kids and interacting with Gertrude and some of the stories she told. It was amazing to hear them at the site they occurred. I then met a Port Monmouth resident named Carly Vena, who became my friend and also instrumental in my study of the Spy House because she had with her original literature and pamphlets written by Gertude herself. She gladly scanned them for me so I could have them. I now had in my possession words from this late caretaker, directly from her and not a story passed down or he-said-she-said. I later found more in the archives of the Atlantic Highlands Historical Society. It was remarkable reading her version of the history.

Also included in this treasure trove was a lengthy 1988 *Coast Magazine* article on the Spy House where Gertrude is interviewed and pictured. It was an eye-opener in 2014, and now ten years later to re-read it all gives me chills. This article contains so many of the well-known legends tied to the property. The same ones you will read if you do an online search, the same that come up in the local newspapers every October, and the same stories that the historian in me now has to say are not true.

Earlier that day, I arrived with Jake to set up for the presentation. One of my other coworkers was there to let us in. I had brought the SB-7 with me and, taking a chance, asked this coworker if there was any chance Jake and I could walk around with it. She shrugged her shoulders and said, "Why not? You have an hour before the talk starts." We walked from room to room with the Spirit Box but, unfortunately, did not hear anything remarkable. Jake and I checked out the basement and found it to be cramped and almost inaccessible—you practically had to crawl to explore it. There were some scattered responses around the house, including hearing the name "George" while up in the attic, but that was pretty much it. This was still a special moment. When the lecture was over, I took out the device and we did a small group session. People were just happy to be there regardless of what happened.

But it was during the lecture that something odd took place. As I was speaking, I kept seeing people in the back of the room looking towards the doorway, some of them with befuddled expressions on their faces. After the third time or so, Jake went out into the hallway to look for himself. I continued the talk and did not think much of it. When it was over, he informed me that he as well as several others in the back heard the faint sound of a baby crying from the next room, but there was no one else in the house at the time. The front door was closed and there did not appear to be anyone outside. No members of the public came into the house during the hour we were inside. I might not have been able to talk about the house being haunted, but at least something decided to make itself known.

As my progression into Spy House lore proceeded following this event, the famous line from the 1962 western *The Man Who Shot Liberty Valance* came to mind, "When legend becomes fact, print the legend." When studying the fields of the paranormal, folklore, or cryptozoology (which I have personally never been into as an investigator), there might not be a truer phrase ever spoken.

People always think they want the truth. They do not. In actuality, they want to be entertained. They want to be scared. They want an adrenaline rush when exploring an allegedly haunted property, and if they are too scared for themselves, they want to hear someone else tell them about it. I will never forget something Jeff told me years ago, before paranormal investigating became so mainstream and normalized like it is today: "People love hearing about what we do because they don't have to do it themselves."

The Spy House is old and in a beautiful location but nothing particularly important ever happened there. It begs one to consider the question that just because something is old, does that make it important to the historical record? If the place was a history museum today and not an "activity center" focused on the local marine life of the Bayshore and the egg-laying habits of horseshoe crabs, there would likely not be enough to talk about if you focused solely on the house itself.

Enter Gertrude Neidlinger. What you are about to read is a concise history of the house according to her, which I have compiled and centralized based on internet sources, hearsay, local lore, and that magazine article from 1988 which truly is a perfect summary: 1) The original portion of the house was built in 1663 by Thomas Whitlock. It is the oldest structure in the entirety of New Jersey, and he was the first permanent resident of Monmouth County. 2) The house contained a tunnel or secret passageway underneath so that the family could hide during Indian raids. 3) Over time, the house was used as a station for marauding pirates, including none other than infamous captains William Kidd and Henry Morgan. They killed and/or tortured their victims in the house. 4) In addition to pirate captains, there was another nameless "sea captain" in the 1600s who owned the home and kept the bodies of the people he killed in the basement. He was described as "extremely evil" and a "killer of children and Indians and worshiped the devil." His spirit is damned to remain trapped in the house until his descendants pray for his soul. 5) Prior to any of this happening, the house was constructed atop the grave of local Indian Chief Popamora, which could be the reason for so much paranormal activity and any ensuing raids. He was a fierce warrior who was angered to see white settlers living on his resting place. 6) There was a Revolutionary War battle fought on the front lawn in 1779. 7) During the Revolution, the house operated as a tavern where the innkeeper would serve liquor to British soldiers, attempting to get them drunk so he could learn their plans and relay such information to George Washington, hence giving us the name Spy House.

Now that is what I call entertainment! I always like to call to mind the age-old saying when researching a history or when experiencing something paranormal myself: "If it's too good to be true, it's probably not." However, Gertrude saw an opportunity here, since when she became involved with the property in the 1970s (it began as a museum in 1972 after operating as a restaurant and bar for nearly forty years previously), it was falling into disrepair. It lasted that way until the early '90s, when Middletown Township finally ousted her and eventually began transferring the house to Monmouth County in 1997. It could be that she began weaving such stories in an attempt to garner attention and, hopefully, financial aid that would save the property. While no major renovations happened during her tenure (and there were also accusations of misappropriating funds and donations by the Spy House Museum Corporation, which cannot be proven), she sure drummed up enough interest which potentially saved the property from being sold and knocked down.

Did the stories help or hurt in the long run? Gertrude managed to take history from the surrounding area and throw it all into this one single location. At a time before internet research could quickly dispel untruths, people apparently ate it up. Even today, when we have the ability to say what is true and what is not, people still tend to believe in the fanciful.

Gertrude was clearly educated on local happenings. She had to be in order to concoct this house's history, which is literally made out of thin air. There was possibly a cabin built on the site in the 1600s, but there is no specific year that can be tied to it. The oldest year that we can see referenced is 1696 when Thomas Whitlock sold the property to Daniel Seabrook, and there is no mention of a structure, just the land.

The actual house, part of which is standing today though heavily changed over the years, was built in approximately the 1720s or later. Why is this important? Because William Kidd and Henry Morgan were both dead by 1701 and pirate activity had long since ceased. There were pirates in the surrounding area, some of them associated with another haunted location that will come in the next chapter, but no famous pirates can be placed there specifically. Gertrude had the existing structure built in 1663, expanded with a second section from 1678–1681, and then the third and final section added by 1703. This is according to her own diagrams. In real life, the house was completed in its current iteration in the mid-1800s, a full century later.

Is it petty to be so concerned with years? It could be assumed that Gertrude did her best in trying to figure out what part was constructed when, and it is not really a big deal that she got it wrong. Here we are in 2023, with all of our modern technology and research capabilities which would have been unavailable to her. However, when you examine the actual application submitted to the National Register of Historic Places by Middletown Township, most of the correct information was already known. Or at least it was more correct than what she was telling people. The date of this application was October 29, 1974. This is important because Gertrude was already active as a member of the museum. It means that she did indeed have access to the right information but chose to present otherwise. The form states, among many other fascinating tidbits, "Family history indicates 17th century settlement, however this house does not appear to go back this far."

In the section regarding the house's period significance, only the boxes marked eighteenth and nineteenth centuries are checked. When it came time to check additional boxes for general areas of significance, it was not "military" they went with, but rather "transportation." Yes, the Spy House was an inn and tavern, but it was not during the American Revolution, but in the late nineteenth and early twentieth centuries when it operated as Bay Side Manor and then The White House. The beach in front of the house was a tourist attraction, with visitors coming from far and wide to swim and relax in the sun. Many towns in the Bayshore experienced heydays as tourist destinations, which may be hard to believe today. This was before the Garden State Parkway, and if one was coming from New York or northern New Jersey, popular stops tended to be Cliffwood Beach, Keansburg, Port Monmouth, Atlantic Highlands, and Highlands.

If there was no tavern where British soldiers were getting drunk, that means there was no spying done from the Spy House at all, an inconvenient and disappointing fact. Any spying done was likely on nearby Garrett's Hill which borders Leonardo and higher elevations further south along the Bayshore. Today it is a residential area with an inconspicuous street named after it and no way for people to know of any historical significance.

Gertrude did mention this point in one of her pieces of literature but tied it into the house by saying spies on the hill would watch what British ships were coming and going and send that to the innkeeper, who would then be prepared to wine and dine the British officers who were about to enter his establishment later on in the evening. Such a story, while untrue, is mundane enough and probably would have been able to keep people interested on its own; however, we also have the story of a battle being fought on the front lawn, which simply never happened.

Something else to consider: if there were conclusively no soldiers, spies, pirates, natives, or evil sea captains and their numerous tortured and murdered victims, what does that say about the psychics who have interacted with such figures on the property over the years? There is also the case of a woman named Penelope Stout who, according to centuries of tradition, was an early settler of the Bayshore. Gertrude mentions her several times in various papers. This Penelope was brutally attacked by Lenape tribesmen who left her for dead in the Sandy Hook area. She managed to survive, and her story became part of local lore as an example of courage and fortitude. However, most historians do not believe she ever existed at all and was simply a tall tale that grew taller with age. Gertrude and her psychics had Penelope not only living at the Spy House in its earliest days but still haunting it in death.

There were skirmishes and activity all over the Bayshore, but nothing ever recorded for Shoal Harbor, which is what Port Monmouth was once known as, with the exception of troops passing through it. In fact, it is hard to find anything about this particular town during the Revolution that does not involve the Spy House, whose only documented connection to the War for Independence was one of the owners, Thomas Seabrook, having fought for the patriot cause along with several family members. That is the only reference to the American Revolution in the entire National Register application.

Gertrude also includes a fun little story about the British turning on the owners of the house and setting it on fire (she lists the house surviving five of them over the centuries). Not only did they attempt to set it ablaze, but they also destroyed all the buckets on the property so that water could not be collected from the bay to put it out. However, the women of the Seabrook family came to the rescue, since it was laundry day, and they took all the wet clothes they could find and smothered the fire.

As for Popamora, who gets lost given the many ins and outs of this history, he really did exist but not much is known about him. His tribal land stretched from the Keansburg area to Navesink, and there is a park named after him in Highlands. His place of burial has been lost to time. But as people know, Indian land and, specifically,

Indian burial grounds are some of the best potential catalysts for hauntings. Gertrude knew this, though she did not really need the help since the house already had so many other sinister spirits residing there. In that 1988 interview, she described a group of children on a school field trip at the house seeing the evil sea captain with their own eyes one day. It appeared to them as a Satanic figure dressed in a black robe with "smoke where his face should have been." The shadow figure Jeff and I saw in the window back in 2010 seems rather boring compared to that.

For the article, she was accompanied by three psychics who gave their commentary on what they were seeing. Psychics, and candle-lit séances, were nothing new to the Spy House, as she encouraged them. Many psychics made a name for themselves by giving tours there with Gertrude. There are tales of all kinds of rituals happening there under her watch, but that might not have been true either. This could have partly been what led to her downfall and eventual transfer of the property. The house was becoming a historical pariah, focused more on ghosts than actual history. In one of my older blog posts, someone did reach out saying that the stories of séances were untrue and only fabricated after the fact to show her as crazy, but we know such séances took place and psychics were integral to the operation.

We see with so many legends that one small story can snowball into something that gains fame. In the case of the Spy House, there are more legends that can be counted, and though they all came from one identifiable source, the effect still goes into place. In 1993, the *New York Times* ran an article titled "Odd Goings-On at the Spy House," which also interviewed Gertude, where she claims she personally never saw a ghost in the house but enjoyed helping her "psychic friends" have access. It was through them that she acquired so many tales.

The article mentions being visited recently by famed paranormal researcher Hans Holzer, all of this helping to encourage the false legends to keep spreading, and nothing to debunk them because if he was truly investigating, he would have uncovered the real facts. Gertrude notes that her entire museum board was comprised of psychics, eight in total, plus her. Some of the familiar stories make their way, but also new ones, including rumrunners from Prohibition and now even pirate treasure being buried on the property. There really was no end.

As for what went on at some of these séances with Gertrude and her gang, they have remained shrouded in mystery over the last half century. In the nearly thirty years since the Spy House's closure and transition, anyone who took part in these has been tight-lipped or faded away into the shadows, with hardly any descriptions appearing online among all the craziness written about this house. That is, it was a mystery until now.

Maybe it was fate, because right as this book reached its final editing stage with only one week left to make changes, a friend of mine, Roseanne Musone Tierney, whose mother worked with Gertrude for many years, informed me that her sister was going through a box of her old documents and found a typewritten transcript of a séance from November 6, 1975 at the Spy House. This was a little over a year after the National Register form was drafted. They thought of me and wanted me to see it. I must say that it takes a lot to cause my jaw to drop, but that was my reaction when I started reading it after she provided me with a copy. Much like my acquisition of some other papers and articles mentioned previously, this was incredibly meaningful to both this chapter and my understanding of the past culture of this building. Once again, this was not hearsay or paraphrasing, but a word-for-word transcript of a Ouija board session that occurred inside.

More shocking to me was reading through some of the names of those present. There were more than twenty people in attendance, including a reporter from the *Asbury Park Press*, but only a few names are actually given, including Gertrude and her brother Trav, two board members, and one more person I ended up working with many years later who I never knew was involved in anything paranormal. This individual knew I was an investigator and this somehow managed to never come up in conversation. Talk about tight-lipped. She is listed as helping with "tape and recording," though this document was typed by someone else based on what was taped. If there were any psychics present, they are not named.

It does not appear that this séance was particularly significant in the long run, but unless someone uncovers a similar document, it is all we have that puts us inside the house at a very exciting time and gives insight into exactly what questions were being asked and what answers "received" by the inquiring group. However, this session did manage to check all the boxes, as various topics which come up include the house being built and lived in by 1664, British soldiers and their alleged attempt to burn the house down, Lenape Indians, tunnels, and spies. Many identities of spirits are also named. Knowing what we know now, it is all the more fascinating to see the origin stories begin to form from what might have been harmless conjecture into outright lies.

In this unpublished six-page document, the people asking the questions are not named either, but it is clearly not Gertrude as whoever is typing makes note that almost every time information perceived as important is given by a spirit through the board, they look to her for confirmation. She and her brother Trav confirm nearly all in question to occur. There is not much room for mystery for this reason, as they have an answer for everything. When a first name is given, the group immediately brings up a last name and asks if it is who they are speaking with, to which the spirit says "Yes" every time. When they start talking to a Will or William, the typist notes that the Neidlingers confirmed that there was a William in the Whitlock family. There are hardly any instances where the questioners press for verifying information, which is unfortunate given that it would not be surprising that a family from the 1700s had someone named William within it.

The group also calls for their own familiar "Spirit Guides" to help them usher in more identities to the forefront. Their names are given as "Sam Lambertson" and "Benjamin Morris," who both lived as mortals in colonial New Jersey, according to Gertrude. All told, there are more than ten different ghosts identified during this session. Some have full names, others only have a first. As someone who has participated in similar séances (though modeled after a Victorian-era method, not a Ouija board), it would be hypocritical for me to totally discount the information given and dismiss it all as fraudulent. But after reading every line of the document, it does appear this was more for entertainment purposes with such a large audience and reporter in attendance.

There is an element of deception, but no one seemed to pick up on it. No new information is learned, since everything is confirmed by the Neidlingers, and there are several historical gaffes which go unnoticed. When Will tells them that he lived in the house in 1826, the question they followed up with moments later was asking if there were any photographs of him. He tells them that there were, but they were all destroyed by the fire the British set during the Revolution. Putting aside the fact that this fire never actually happened, one does not have to be a historian or Rhodes Scholar to understand the multiple issues with such an assertion. The first photograph in history was not taken until the 1820s and photography itself did not become commonplace until decades later. How then could Will have his photo destroyed during the American Revolution which ended by 1783? It is possible that someone could have been alive during this time period and still alive in 1826, but that is as far as this situation can be stretched. The rest is laughable, especially coming from people professing to be historians and caretakers of a historic site.

The conversation then spirals into the familiar. The fire occurred over part of the house that had a tunnel (which never existed) underneath and the spirit begins to tell them of children "hiding in a hole," which is ascertained to be an old well, and that they were screaming because the British were after them. Hardly anything that occurred in this entire document could have actually happened. The séance winds down with those in attendance asking the spirit, now their friendly guide Benjamin Morris, to make the room cold. It is noted that a few minutes later, two participants noticed a change in temperature. Of course they did.

Gertrude's run finally came to an end in 1993, shortly after that *New York Times* article came out which may or may not have been a coincidence. Apparently, there was great controversy in her removal or forced resignation. The township was concerned not only with wrong history being told, but also the séances which were done by candlelight and posed a fire hazard. At one of my paranormal lectures at Brookdale Community College, when I was in the midst of compiling this information, I met one of the members of the county who was active in her removal. She told me point blank, "There are no ghosts, no pirates, no spies. She was an actress, a very good actress." While I still believe the house is haunted, this person was right about her acting ability, and further research indicates Gertude was a concert soprano and actress—someone used to giving performances. Her brother Trav, also involved in the management of the museum for many years, was an artist and painter.

In between her removal and the Monmouth County Park System acquiring the property in 1997, the house remained closed, with all of the many artifacts and exhibits locked inside. This included antique fishing equipment and furniture, clothing, mannequins, tools, and whale bones. The County swiftly wanted everything removed to "avoid becoming involved with any ownership controversies." The bulk of it went into a self-storage unit in Hazlet before being given to the Heath Farm in Middletown on Harmony Road. There it remains, barely seeing the light of day for over twenty-five years.

Additional items were donated and loaned to local historical societies and museums, including the Murray Farmhouse at Poricy Park, Longstreet Farm at Holmdel Park, and the Strauss Mansion Museum, Atlantic Highlands Historical Society headquarters. Shortly before locking this manuscript before publication, I happened upon a list of what came to the AHHS in the archives. This will be discussed in the last chapter.

There are multiple sources which indicate that Gertude did end up having a lawsuit filed against either the County or Middletown Township for possession of the items and surprisingly won the case. She either died shortly after or, in typical dramatic fashion, the very next day after the verdict depending on who you ask. Her death, compounded with no one able to properly disperse the items which were now legally hers, have led them to end up in a limbo of sorts.

By 1998, the MCPS was firmly entrenched at the Spy House, most of the items had been removed, and Gertrude Neidlinger was dead. In reading through some of these documents, it is incredible how quickly everything transpired. In the blink of an eye, a legendary museum became a shell of itself, only to spend decades trying to be reinvented like a phoenix rising from the ashes of some great calamity. To many people, this reinvention has not been a positive one, since it shattered the stories and memories that they held so dear to themselves for so many years, especially of a figure they loved and enjoyed being around. As a human being, I relate. As a historian, it was necessary.

And there I was in 2014, conducting a mini paranormal investigation at the very place where the paranormal caused so much harm (though all of this was unknown to me at the time). In the moment, I thought it was amazing to be the first person allowed to conduct a ghost-themed event at the Spy House since the Gertrude era came to an end. Thinking about it now, the irony is not lost on me as I have personally used the paranormal to fundraise tens of thousands of dollars for historic preservation over the years, beginning at the Proprietary House and, in more recent years, for the Atlantic Highlands Historical Society.

To me, it has always been an effective way of not just bringing in much-needed donations, but hooking people with interesting information in the hopes that they will become frequent visitors or patrons for the historical aspects. The one difference is that my team and I do not make up or invent a history in order to create interest. I see the duality of Gertrude's situation and what she caused. The historian in me is frustrated at the energy it takes to have a serious conversation about the Spy House and to inform people of the truth when, for their entire lives, they have believed that all of these fantastic things happened there. However, I can also see her as someone who maybe saved the old house (on prime real estate) from being bought by someone without preservation intentions, razed, and turned into waterfront condos overlooking the New York City skyline. Do we admonish her, or thank her? Or is it a little bit of both?

Even gradually gaining this knowledge, I am still drawn to visit there once a year (usually in October), during which some members of the team will join me for a walk around the property with some of our devices. We will look in the windows to see if we can spot anything moving like Jeff and I did on that inspiring night all those years ago. My last visit with the intent to investigate was in 2018, when Jake and I went on Halloween afternoon to test out his new Ovilus III, which can be seen on many of the ghost hunting shows on TV. It is a small, computerized device, about the size of a television remote, that has a database of 10,000 words programmed inside it. Nearby entities then use their energy to manipulate this word bank and communicate with investigators.

The Ovilus III has been very hit and miss over the years, but we have had luck by turning it on something called "phonetic mode," where it does not use the words but rather speaks like a person, supposedly, through spirit manipulation. Most of the time what we hear is gibberish, but that afternoon, we heard what we thought was "Spy House" after I had opened the session by asking them to, "Please say 'Spy House' to confirm that you can hear us." About thirty seconds later, we were cursed out with extreme undebatable clarity. Like the SB-7, profanity helps advance the case since the

F-word is not part of the computer program, and we were not on that setting to begin with. The rest of our investigation was pretty quiet.

In Gertrude's own words, there are twenty-four spirits that call the Spy House home, with many more coming and going. Perhaps she herself still walks the halls, but we will likely never be able to confirm that for sure, as chances of any future paranormal programs are not currently possible. I consider myself extremely lucky to have had the chance, though it was a small one. Over the years, as I have worked with different program coordinators for the MCPS (including several more presentations of "Haunted History" at different locations), I am always asked if I have any new ideas or if there is anything I would be interested in presenting. One of my steady answers has always been to let me conduct a fundraiser paranormal investigation at the Spy House, from which I would not ask to be paid—just being inside would be enough. But it never gets anywhere. I have to admire their steadfastness, because in a day and age where the paranormal could generate so much income, they have yet to back down, and understandably so.

The damage over the years has been done, and no matter how much they try to shut it down, or people like me try to write the facts, the majority will always believe in the pirates, spies, and that evil sea captain. History aside, belief in the "haunted" Spy House is harmless enough. I just want people to have the correct history behind it. So take a drive there at night. Walk the property under the light of the moon. Stick your flashlights in those windows. You just never know what you might uncover, or what path it might lead you on.

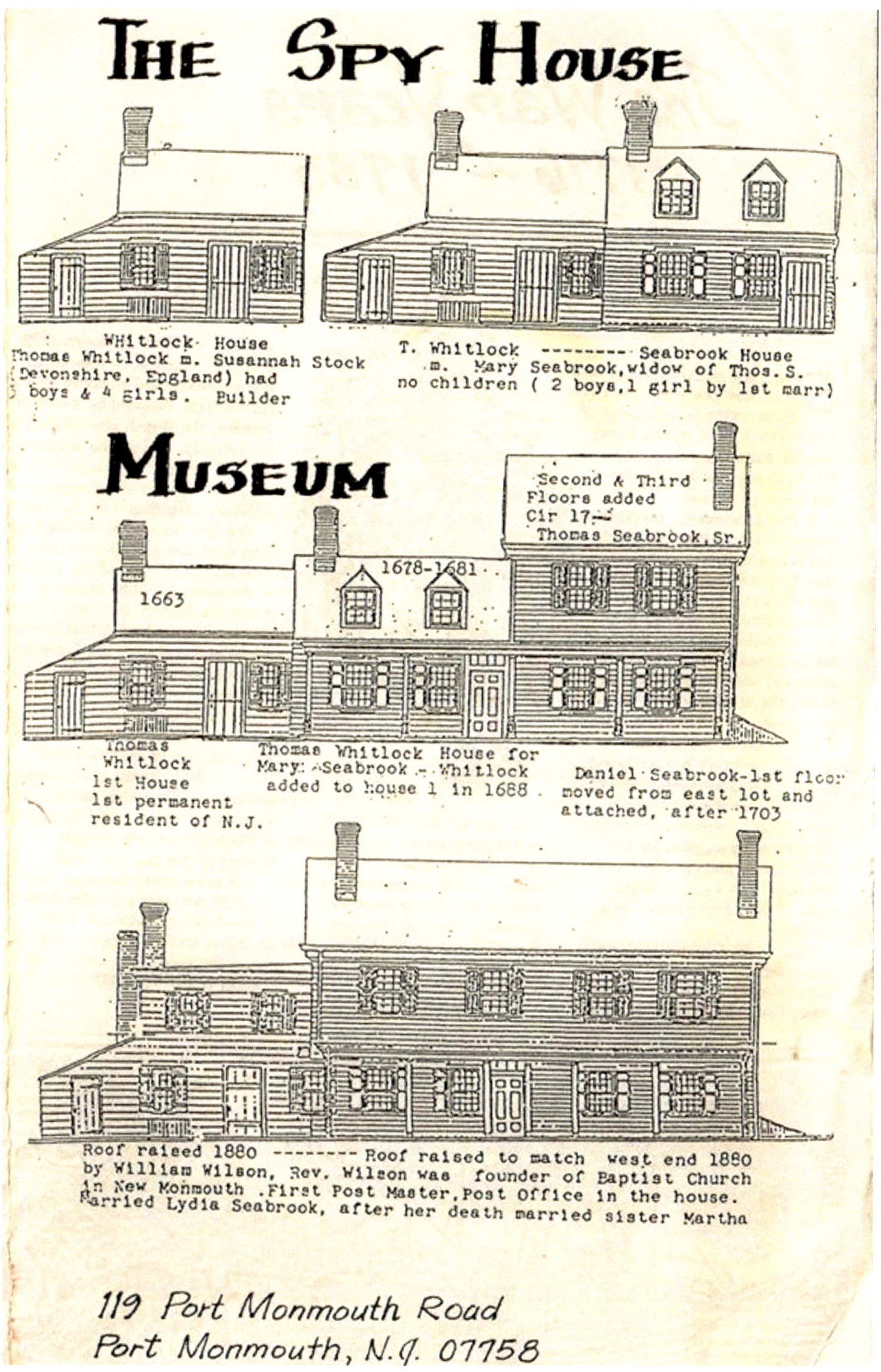


Gertrude Neidlinger's own diagram showing her version of when the Spy House was constructed and added on to. (*Spy House Museum Corporation*)

*Left:* A young Gertrude Neidlinger, pictured here in the 1940s or '50s when she was a singer. Internet searches for her image only churn up a few results, with most of them when she was of advanced age. (*Montclair Public Library*)

*Below:* The house, as seen in 1896 when it was a private residence. Pictured here are two of the owners: Benjamin Griggs and his wife, Martha Seabrook. (*Monmouth County Park System*)

A 1915 postcard showing the building when it was Bay Side Manor. The negative of this image was flipped, since the smaller section would be on the left side if facing the house from this direction. (*Monmouth County Park System*)

The Spy House in 1974, as the Shoal Harbor Museum, after spending decades as a tavern and restaurant. (*National Parks Service*)

This is the side of the house which faces the water. "Abigail's Window" is allegedly on the second floor, the second window in from the right.

*Opposite above:* This photo dates to the 1950s and the building's use as a tavern and store, when the only spirits present were of the drinking kind. (*Monmouth County Historical Association*)

*Opposite below:* The Spy House in September 2023. A new roof had been under construction in the previous weeks and was finally completed.

# 5

# SHARKS AND PIRATES AND HORSES, OH MY!

## ROSE HILL CEMETERY, MATAWAN, AND BROOKDALE COMMUNITY COLLEGE, LINCROFT

On July 14, 1916, the body of an eleven-year-old boy named Lester Stillwell was pulled from the waters of Matawan Creek, where he had gone missing two days earlier. The area he had visited with his friends was a popular swimming hole. Though the Jersey Shore had experienced two shark attacks in the previous two weeks, occurring in Beach Haven and, later, Spring Lake, there was not much cause for concern as the creek was several miles inland. The thought would not have crossed anyone's mind, though several witnesses believed they saw a shark in that very water days before Stillwell went missing.

Written off as hysteria, or mistaken for a long wooden log, the children went swimming as they would have on any other day. Stillwell began to scream, writhe in pain, and then vanished beneath the surface. Though the group he was with thought they saw a fin protruding out from the water, Stillwell was an epileptic and the possibility that he was experiencing a seizure also had to be considered. Townspeople were quickly assembled and made their way to the banks of the creek. One of the men in this group was named Stanley Fisher, who immediately jumped into the water to find Stillwell. In front of several people, the shark that could not exist and certainly could not make it so far inland emerged and bit Fisher in the leg so severely that he eventually bled to death, succumbing several hours later.

Putting two and two together, with the combination of sightings and actual attacks that happened further south, the Jersey Shore appeared to be under siege by what locals dubbed "The Matawan Man Eater." The simple act of going for a dip on a hot summer afternoon resulted in two dead young men. There would be a third victim later that day, as approximately a half hour after Stillwell and Fisher were attacked, another boy, Joseph Dunn, who was swimming farther down the creek by one of the docks, felt a sharp pain in his left leg. Stunned and perplexed, he was aghast to see a shark attempting to devour him.

His friend and brother who were swimming with him began to literally wrestle his body out of the shark's mouth. His leg was down the shark's throat by this point, yet

80

they managed to dislodge him. However, it was nearly stripped of all flesh in the process. Dunn managed to survive the ordeal, but was likely traumatized for life, telling an interviewer that he was sure the shark was going to swallow him whole.

Unlike the previous attacks, which occurred in the ocean on expansive beaches, the target area in Matawan was smaller, and not as deep. It was possible that the shark might still be trapped in the narrow waters. Straight out of a Hollywood movie, the town gathered up everything short of torches and pitchforks in an attempt to find the "Man Eater." There are photographs of people in row boats, sailing through the creek, with shotguns aimed at the water. Others thought that guns would be futile against such a large beast and began setting off dynamite in strategic points in the creek.

Such an incident would have been unconscionable in 1916. It made headlines in newspapers across the country. Even today, the thought of a shark attack is terrifying, though one seems to occur every summer with varying levels of damage inflicted to the victim. And we have already been desensitized by horror films such as *Jaws*, on which this attack was partly based. But to the people of Matawan, this would have come from nowhere. There was hardly any understanding of sharks at all; in fact, this series of attacks on the Jersey Shore helped to elevate the shark to a level of equal parts popularity and fear in a matter of days.

Today, you can visit the area near where the attack occurred. Some of the swamps are visible from the Garden State Parkway. Trying to imagine a gigantic shark killing people in such an unsuspecting place may be as eye-opening today as it was a century ago.

I first learned of the attacks altogether as a child, but in the last place you would ever expect such a history lesson: a restaurant. There was a dining establishment and bar in Matawan, not far from the creek, that operated as The Poet's Inn from 1961 until the early 2000s, when it was sold and changed names. It is still a restaurant today and looks much the same. Strangely enough, the back of the menu contained a history of the 1916 Matawan shark attacks and featured copies of original newspaper clippings. I was always obsessed with history and read the little stories every time I ate there with my parents, which was several times a year.

The restaurant itself was also historic in a way. Poet Philip Freneau lived on or near the property and it was named as a tribute to the man who had been christened by some as "The Poet of the American Revolution." Had this place still been around now, I would have liked to ask the owner what made them put such a story there. And no, there was no shark meat on the menu—that would have been a delicious irony.

But what would such an incident be without lore? Both Stillwell and Fisher would go on to be buried at Rose Hill Cemetery in Matawan. However, over the years, stories have sprung up that Stillwell in particular is not at rest and keeps watch over his grave. It has persisted that when trying to photograph the headstone, images will come out blurry. This can be easily debunked, as I have many pictures of the grave. I do, however, wonder where this story came from. Sure, Stillwell was a child whose life was snuffed out in the blink of an eye, but Fisher too was young (twenty-four years old) and killed in a similar manner, with much of his whole life still left ahead of him. There are no stories of him.

The thought of a cemetery being haunted has conflicted me over the years. Though the land for any cemetery may contain thousands of bodies, no one died there, and death itself does not necessarily mean a place would be haunted. If there was a spirit, either happy or sad, it is my belief that if they choose to hang around, it would be at a place much more meaningful than what is left of their mortal remains. But as for Stillwell and this story, perhaps, it is not so much about the who as it is the where. Rose Hill has long been connected to not only paranormal activity, but pirates as well.

About a decade ago, I became friends with the late Tom Burke who was a Matawan-based historian, author, Civil War expert, and then the president of the New Jersey Civil War Heritage Association. I told him I was going to be in his neck of the woods one afternoon, with a few friends investigating Rose Hill because of some of the articles I had read online about it. He called me up immediately and said he wanted to come. I asked if we could interview him on camera at the cemetery first, which he agreed.

Before we filmed, I asked point blank, "Is this place haunted?" He said, "Oh, there's a lot going on here," and added that he had heard all kinds of stories about strange things happening at night—not of the paranormal variety, but visitors getting up to all kinds of unholy activities. Maybe he was exaggerating, maybe not. But he was more of an academic than a ghost hunter, and so I paid attention to what he said.

In order to understand Rose Hill, we also have to understand the changing landscape. For the Jersey Bayshore, which was quite populous, Matawan was more isolated. The creeks that are there today, where the shark attack occurred and also nearby, used to be a lot wider and was the site of a booming shipping economy where goods were transported through Matawan and also Keyport, the neighboring town. You would not get that vibe today.

Also impossible to picture is Rose Hill itself standing out to the point where it would be a landmark. With so many tall trees dotting the area, and numerous houses and businesses, you likely would not be able to spot it from afar. But once upon a time ago, there was an exceptionally tall tree located at the top of the hill, which was rumored to be used by Captain Kidd as he allegedly navigated the same waters that witnessed the deaths of Stillwell and Fisher centuries later.

William Kidd and Henry Morgan undoubtedly did not step foot in the Spy House nor the land surrounding it, but they were sailing the waters of the Jersey Bayshore. It might not be a coincidence that there is part of Cliffwood Beach today named Morgan. According to Burke and so many others online, the popular legend is that as Kidd came and went on his many journeys up and down the east coast, he paused near Matawan and buried some of his treasure where Rose Hill currently is. This would have been a much safer place than the stereotypical image of a treasure chest being buried right on a beach which was much more accessible.

The area was purported to be a Lenape Indian burial ground, which white settlers eventually turned into a cemetery of their own (though it was not officially a cemetery until the 1800s). Kidd would have found this to be the perfect place to bury treasure, as not many people attempting to find it would have the gall to dig up a cemetery. The tall tree, which may or may not exist today (it might just be blending in with the rest of the trees), was Kidd's navigational marker so he could tell where he was sailing. It is not determined if Kidd ever returned to this treasure, but the rumors of it being there will never die. There are also no stories of Kidd's ghost being at Rose Hill either—if his treasure was there, would he not want to watch over it?

There are many locations up and down the Jersey Shore which supposedly are the final resting place for buried treasure. Manasquan, Barnegat, Toms River, and Brigantine all have legends and stories associating Captain Kidd, his treasure, and a burial in their town. I cannot dismiss those stories as false, just as I would hope that historians further down in South Jersey would not dismiss the possibility of a Matawan burial to be true either. Gold coins were rumored to have washed up in Cliffwood Beach some years ago, but it was not enough to be considered treasure, and with the number of ships that came and went (and sunk) in these waters over the centuries, they literally could have come from anywhere.

Tom never told me his opinion on whether or not he believed Kidd really did bury anything at Rose Hill, but he was open to the possibility. In our short tour with him that afternoon, Tom's knowledge spread to his main area of expertise which was the American Civil War. We happened to be standing next to the graves of two of such soldiers for the video. The first was Daniel Provost, who was killed in one of Ulysses S. Grant's ill-fated charges at the battle of Cold Harbor in Virginia. Replacing him in the ranks as he fell was his brother, William, who soon met the same fate. Their bodies managed to be sent home to this cemetery where they rest today. Stories of tragedies cannot be enough to make a haunting. Every cemetery has people whose lives were cut short, either naturally or through violent means, but most cemeteries manage to remain serene and peaceful, and not points of intrigue for paranormal investigations.

It could be the land that is the draw because of its unique situation. It is not flat but a hill. There is a road that winds around, taking you to the top. As you make your way up, there are vaults and crypts built into the hillside. Some of them you are able to look inside, either by putting your head up to the door or by sticking your camera through any windows. It can be tricky investigating a cemetery that is still actively used, because one does not want to seem insensitive. For that reason, we avoid areas with recent graves and tend to stick to the parts that seem like they have been forgotten or are simply old enough that we would hope to not be bothering anyone.

The crypts lend a creepy feeling, no doubt, as does the solitude. Despite being surrounded by a residential neighborhood on all sides, there is an eerie quiet that descends upon visitors, especially up at the top. For a moment, you may temporarily forget that you are located in such a densely populated area. If you go right around sunset, as the darkness falls, the atmosphere seems almost ethereal. I have never had any feelings other than peace and tranquility at Rose Hill, so it surprises me to read stories online of people who were scared out of their wits while walking around at night. Others have captured what they call "ectoplasm" on camera, a term I tend to avoid given its humorous connotations from *Ghostbusters*.

There is also a zombie buried at Rose Hill. I read a little snippet online one day and asked Tom about it. He smiled and said, "I won't tell you where or what it is. You have to find it. But yes, there is a Zombie interred there." Brett and another co-investigator Hunter Dillon, who joined us in 2015, and I searched the cemetery for what seemed like hours. We finally discovered the etching "Zombie" on a large, well-maintained grave for the Hulsart family. There were several names on the large stone. Now, we knew this was not an actual zombie but were definitely curious. Was it a prank? Did they name their child (due to the age on the stone) something really off-the-wall? We took it so seriously that it never occurred to us that it was the family dog whom the Hulsarts loved so much that they wanted him to rest beside them for all eternity. This grave has become an attraction itself.

Only one picture ever taken at an investigation at Rose Hill that I have been on churned up something odd. Jake had an image where in the upper left portion was a gigantic pink blob. It was dark outside, so it was not sunlight. There was nothing reflective in view that could have caused a burst of light. My final attempt to rule it out as paranormal was suggesting that maybe his fingertip was over the lens of the camera, but it is entirely see-through. If it is an orb, it may be the biggest I have personally seen in an image.

Aside from that, we have conducted several investigations over the years. Nothing ever scared us. We got many SB-7 responses but nothing that seemed to be relevant to what was going on. In 2018, we took Jake's Ovilus III and set it down at the base of one of the crypts. At the end of the session, after not speaking to us clearly on phonetic mode, it told us "goodbye." More interesting than this video, though, was one of the comments that we received on it. Someone recognized the mausoleum we were at from when they visited as a child in the 1970s. They were told by an older caretaker that it had to be cemented and secured because someone had broken in, entered one of the coffins, and dumped the bones on the ground. I had not seen this information anywhere else, so perhaps it is true. Well, the person being told this is true, but whether the caretaker was relaying the correct information or just trying to scare them will never be known.

The ghosts, if there are any, never divulged the information of Kidd's buried treasure. Maybe it is not, nor ever was, at Rose Hill Cemetery. Maybe it never was at any of the obvious shore towns either. Maybe Kidd never buried it at all, but instead took it with him to church.

We are now going to veer about 11 miles to the southeast for the continuation of this story. A year after I started lecturing for Brookdale Community College, I was asked if I wanted to run any educational summer camps for middle and high school students on campus. I proposed a couple of ideas, which included battle tactics and war, as well as politics and debate. Both were approved and immensely popular. My supervisor at the time asked if I had any more ideas. I was hesitant to suggest a camp on the paranormal, but I figured I had nothing to lose. By this time, I was giving paranormal lectures to adults at Brookdale, and it always drew younger audiences than my history ones. A paranormal camp ended up getting approved as well.

Each of these lasted one week, from Monday to Friday, and were almost as long as a school day. They were confined to campus classrooms and were educational in nature. A few days after I proposed the idea for a paranormal investigating camp, I had second thoughts. "How am I going to get a full week out of this?" I said to myself. I then figured that if I expanded on my original presentations, showed videos of past investigations from our YouTube, and then went into more folklore subjects, that would be enough to stretch into a week. I also planned on doing demonstrations of the equipment so the participants could see what ghost hunting was all about.

But all of this in a nondescript community college classroom? That ran the risk of becoming boring fast, especially since I was not expecting to find anything. While later years saw the group of participants increase in number (the first year had only eight, but it swelled to nearly twenty within two years) and the college rented a bus to take us on field trips to the Strauss Mansion, of which I was a board member, that first year we had to make do with what we had, which was not much.

Right at the beginning of the first camp, I told the students two things: 1) There was no guarantee of paranormal activity to be experienced, and 2) If anything does happen, it is genuine. This is not a "haunted fun house" where my assistant (who was Patrick) and I are going to bang on walls or create parlor tricks to scare you. The kids were eager to get started.

At around the same time that I was preparing for this camp, I was also designing a paranormal workshop for adults at Brookdale. This took my original lecture where I told stories of my paranormal experiences and added a how-to section along with a demonstration and investigation within the classroom. As history has always been important to me in these talks, this new program would include a history of the property so that we might direct our questions specifically to whatever spirits may be around. Even if not directly tied to the property, sometimes opening communication can draw in entities from the surrounding area who are looking for someone to talk to.

Like my thoughts on the camp, I did not think the campus would be haunted. Aside from several coworkers telling me of being "creeped out" late at night while working alone in their offices, there were no specific stories of paranormal encounters. This could be because no one has ever truly looked (and I maintain that Patrick and I and our first participants that year were the first people to investigate the campus) or that it just was not haunted.

I decided that I needed to look farther than the college itself, because there clearly were no dead professors walking the hallways. The property, though, was much more interesting. It had belonged to the Thompson family in its recent history, and the neighboring Thompson Park is named after them. They were breeders of horses, including the winner of the 1915 Kentucky Derby, and the land was named Brookdale Farms. In the centuries prior, the land was known as the "Brookdale Triangle" because of how it was situated, and it was likely inhabited by the Lenape Indians and no doubt passed through by both British and Continental Soldiers. The Dutch and English had also settled on the land. Deer were plentiful in the thick forests, and there was salmon to be fished out of the bordering Swimming River Reservoir.

The east side of the campus is abutted by Phalanx Road, named after the North American Phalanx, which was located within walking distance from Brookdale. It was there that the followers of philosopher Charles Fourier attempted to create an egalitarian utopian society under the leadership of Albert Brisbane. They built a socialist commune with the goal of creating a literal utopia. The community had its own government and economy, and membership was strictly controlled. Dormitories, dining rooms, a school, numerous shops, and a mill were constructed on 673 acres of farmland beginning in 1844. However, this heaven on earth wrought with equality and happiness only managed to last ten years, as debates over issues on slavery and whether the community should be more religiously based caused a split. The buildings managed to last until the 1970s, when a fire destroyed every trace. There is only a small historic marker remaining.

If that was not enough, there is also a pirate connection, again to Captain Kidd. Historians have debated his involvement in the Bayshore, and that also extends to possible movements farther inland. For years, people have claimed that Christ Church in Shrewsbury and Christ Church in Middletown (which were both one parish at that time) were partially financed by Kidd (who also helped to build a church in Manhattan). Adding to this was his cohort William Leeds being a founding member and also a respectable citizen. Where Brookdale sits now was once Leedsville, and William allegedly once had a "sea chest" that he left to the church in Shrewsbury, which has since gone missing into the shadows of history. Did pirate money help finance a church?

Like the Spy House and Rose Hill, we cannot specifically confirm that Kidd was at any of these places, each being more unlikely or impossible than the other. But the introduction of William Leeds into this story may be the missing piece, since he was real and is buried at the Christ Church in Shrewsbury. Though inland, the area was rumored to be a place of refuge for pirates and privateers seeking to get away from the dangers of the Bayshore. But like many of these legends, it is just that: a rumor. Leeds' involvement with Kidd is viewed the same way.

Much of this information comes from a little-known 1927 publication titled *The Story of Middletown* by Ernest Mandeville, which reads with so many exciting tales of pirates and battles that it makes one contemplate if it was written by someone who was related to Gertrude Neidlinger. However, the preface does say that the book is based a lot on what was told to him, and that he did not consider himself a "worthy historian." Consensus by other historians on this book is similar to my views on the real history of the Spy House: the stories may be based partially in fact of events to occur elsewhere but not exactly the area it says.

Oral histories themselves can sometimes turn into a game of telephone, depending on how many mouths they have passed through and over how many years. Stories of pirates so far inland and attending or building a church might have a basis in truth. Maybe a parishioner was once a pirate. Maybe there was a "chest" of some sort that may or may not have held valuables. Most families would have had a large wooden box in their possession to keep items important to them. Either explanation is innocent but also has room to grow, expand, and become filled-in with much more interesting information by storytellers.

Since we will probably never be able to fully confirm or fully deny any of these pirate connections, it may be just as likely that such elusive treasure is buried at Brookdale Community College as it is at Rose Hill or any of the other numerous possible locations. In any case, it made our ensuing paranormal investigations a lot more interesting because there was so much potential. When we turn that Spirit Box on, who will come through? A Revolutionary War soldier? A member of a utopian society? Captain Kidd or William Leeds with the location of their treasure? Someone who worked with horses when the land was owned by the Thompsons? We ended up getting quite a few spirits to come through over the years, but most would be workers from Brookdale Farms, or so they said.

We were always hoping to talk to Geraldine Thompson (*née* Morgan), who with her husband, Lewis, operated Brookdale Farms as a successful breeding ground which was started by his father Colonel William Thompson. The pair made a phenomenally wealthy couple, and she became much beloved and earned the nickname "First Lady of New Jersey" because of her philanthropic activities, many of which were ahead of their time such as being devoted to healthcare, prison reform, and institutions for the care of the mentally ill. Socially and politically savvy, she was friends with Eleanor Roosevelt, and played baseball with Franklin prior to his polio diagnosis. She had a love of sports and driving her car at high speeds around the property.

Lewis spent most of his time at their other home in Georgia, while Geraldine and the children preferred Brookdale. She was seen as a loving and caring figure, not just to her children but also to the children of their servants. She preferred there to be no social or color barriers between her own and those of the staff, and all of them were seen as her first priority. There is no telling how many servants and stable hands for the horse barns, which were removed and turned into blocks of classrooms and lecture halls, there would have been. She passed away in 1967, her death described as peaceful because she said she was ready since most of her family was already predeceased. She had continued to run a successful breeding business for many years after the death of her husband.

The historian in me wanted to talk to this remarkable woman and ask what she thinks of the property being used for education as opposed to horse-racing. Does she still walk the grounds, looking out for the young students of Brookdale? Is she proud of her accomplishments? I also wanted to ask what she thought about the fire in 2006 that destroyed the original Thompson Mansion, which was rebuilt to an almost identical copy years later. While I did ask, there were no answers, at least not from her. It would appear she is at peace.

However, when the camp finally began and it came time to try a Spirit Box session, we were not quite prepared for the number of responses and names that we would be receiving. Though the classroom did not provide a creepy setting, it did allow for a strictly controlled environment. They gave me a room that did not have a camp happening on either side, so it would be quiet. We were on the second floor, which meant there would be no noises above us, either. Except for a small skylight, we could control light sources and reflections. The temperature would be constant. There were no creaky floorboards. These are all the items to consider when investigating a place for the first time, as you have to be prepared for everything that can cause human error when determining if an incident is paranormal.

The room was large enough, and the group small enough, that we could spread out. We set up a table with the SB-7 and also K-2 and EMF detectors. We could position ourselves to be far enough away to prevent a false reading of an energy spike that can be caused by being too close to a cell phone.

Through our questions, we came into contact with four identifiable spirits: Lester, Peter, Joe, and Tom. As we probed further, wondering who they were, they described themselves as stable hands who worked at Brookdale Farms. Geraldine did not reach out to us, but they knew who she was. One by one they described themselves in bits and pieces coming through the static. Lester remained with us on and off for the duration of the camp, and joining us in ensuing years. He told us that he and his fellow workers were of African American descent, were in their teens, and enjoyed working with the horses. It was also the late 1800s, as they were able to confirm what year it was (by us asking one year at a time until we got an affirmative reaction).

By this time, the camp was so active, with frequent K-2 and EMF spikes, that I no longer was being pessimistic about finding anything. Lester joined us and tried to fill in more of the missing pieces. The skeptic in me still wondered. Everything was happening so fast, which is unusual for investigating a place for the first time. We turned on our devices and got immediate answers, some of them full sentences. When one participant asked if the spirits went to school, and later asked what they learn there, a voice came through saying, "Do your homework, kid." Patrick was called an "idiot" twice, in what seemed like a playful manner. The next year, at the same camp with different students, one of them standing next to Patrick (and unaware of any of the previous year's sessions) asked the spirits if they knew Patrick's name. The same voice as the year before responded, "Idiot."

There were cold spots present in this classroom that came and went. The controlled environment and knowing where the air vents were located was helpful in confirming if any coldness was paranormal, and not just a draft. Patrick asked if there was a spirit standing next to him because he felt cold, and immediately, we heard, "I was."

But I kept getting drawn back to Lester. Was he really a former worker on the Thompson Estate? We have learned through years of investigating that some ghosts will say anything just to get attention and keep you speaking to them. There likely were hundreds of workers over the years, and records of them have long-since vanished. I did some digging on the history of Brookdale Farms and was led to a small history PDF on the college's website. It was mostly standard information on the history of the farms and use for horses, but towards the end was a picture that gave me chills. From 1906, there was an assembly of twenty-one stable hands and groomers posing for a photograph in front of one of the barns. Almost every single one of them appeared to be in their twenties or teenagers, and every single one African American. Was Lester one of them?

So many investigations become dead ends. A spirit makes themselves known, tells investigators a little bit about his or herself, and then they lead to absolutely nowhere unable to be confirmed. And no, we cannot confirm Lester was in this photo or existed at all, but the fact that we were told that the spirits communicating with us were African American teenagers and this picture proved such people actively worked on the property was a big step in this becoming an actual investigation, not just try to kill time to finish out the week.

The kids were fascinated and surprised, but so was I. Most, if not all, of them had never done anything like this before, and I had to stress that hardly ever is a series of investigations so fruitful in trying to confirm a fact. The picture was soon printed out and used as a trigger object during the rest of the investigations that first week, and also in years to come. It usually draws out K-2 spikes, as levels on the meter have reached red when near this picture.

Maybe Geraldine truly was as nice as everyone said, and Brookdale Farms was as beautiful and important, for so many spirits to continue residing peacefully. They might still be in their time, seeing the large barns and horses, and maybe totally unaware of the college campus we were standing in. Only one spirit ever got snippy with us, which was in the form of an EVP recorded by Patty at one of my nighttime paranormal workshops for adults in 2018. As I was wrapping up the program (my voice can be heard in the background), a female voice whispers "Get up … get out." This was said just as everyone was about to leave. Maybe she was tired of us bothering her.

Patty had joined our team two years earlier after attending several of my public investigations at the Strauss Mansion. She managed to capture so many EVP recordings, which are far greater and rarer evidence than SB-7 responses, that I asked her to join the team. The majority of her captures will be discussed in the last chapter of this book. This was one of the first profound EVPs we had ever gotten at another location.

Future paranormal camps continued for another five years, all with slight changes. One year, we were invited to investigate the Monmouth Museum, which was on the grounds. It was not active with paranormal energy, but still a neat opportunity, nonetheless. They were all more active than I thought they ever would be when I started them, but none were as eye-opening as that very first one.

How a simple search for pirates ended up taking twists and turns through shark attacks, farmland, and then a college campus. That is why incorporating history into paranormal investigations and the study of folklore is so important because you just never know where it will lead you. It is also important to note that debunking anything is not meant to ruin the fun. Believing stories and checking out some of these locations is a rite of passage that should be enjoyed, even if the reasons for bringing someone there are not true. There will be no greater example of this than our next location.

Matawan locals hunt for the "Man-Eater" in the shallow waters not far from where the attacks occurred. (*Matawan Historical Society*)

Dynamite is detonated in an attempt to kill the shark, or at least cause it to stir so that it might be more easily found. The shark was likely long gone by then. (*Matawan Historical Society*)

The hunt for the shark became an attraction, with locals arriving at the banks of the creeks and swamps to see what was happening. This picture was likely taken shortly before or after the dynamite was exploded. (*Matawan Historical Society*)

Captain William Kidd has long been associated with Rose Hill Cemetery, the Spy House, Christ Church, and countless locations up and down the Jersey Shore. But how many of those places could he actually have visited? (*James Thornhill*)

A mural commemorating the 1916 Matawan shark attack was painted by a local artist a short distance away. Seeing the area today makes it even more incredible that such an event occurred there.

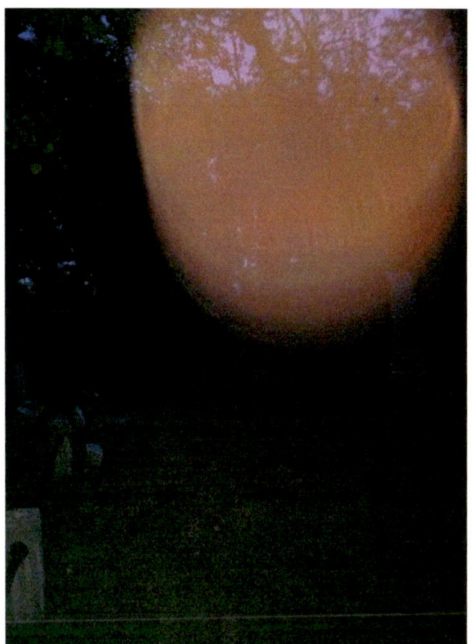

*Right:* An enormous orb (which some people have likened to "ectoplasm") captured at Rose Hill in 2013 or 2014. (*Jake Reid*)

*Below:* The Hulsart family's grave at Rose Hill. Their beloved dog Zombie rests with them for eternity.

The crypt of Abram J. Vreeland, which was allegedly the victim of vandalism in the 1970s.

Some of the crypts at Rose Hill blend into the hillside and become covered with vines and foliage, leading to a spookier feel when walking around.

Fall is the perfect time to visit Rose Hill for photography. Perhaps you will find it as peaceful as I have on my many visits

One of the last surviving buildings of the North American Phalanx in Lincroft. It eventually burned down in 1972. Nothing remains of this once thriving community. (*National Parks Service*)

An undated letter showing one of the barns from the Thompson Estate that would later be converted into part of the college campus. (*Brookdale Community College*)

An 1898 photograph of the original Thompson Mansion. It has since burned down and was rebuilt in an identical manner. (*Monmouth County Park System*)

Stable hands and workers on the Thompson Estate in 1906. (*Brookdale Community College*)

Geraldine Thompson poses on the porch of her mansion. (*Brookdale Community College*)

**6**

# A DRIVE DOWN WHIPPORWILL ROAD

## WHIPPORWILL VALLEY ROAD AND COOPER ROAD, MIDDLETOWN

Witches, Satanism, the Ku Klux Klan—all of these are associated with a single small road in Middletown, which measures just over a mile long. There are several such "haunted" roads in New Jersey, and probably all over the country. What draws people to these locations? Furthermore, what pulls them into these tall tales without wondering if they have one iota of truth? For the people of this area, Whipporwill is a generational affair.

My friends and I would drive down it at night while in high school. Then, in college, Brett and I took a more investigative approach and attempted to compile all the legends for our own amusement. We shot a video and wrote a blog post. Then I went back with Jake a year later for Haunted Travels, and Patrick a few years after that for Ghosts on the Coast. In each instance I recounted the many tales to our viewers, but it was beginning to become dull, because there was just nothing to find while driving down this road. Finally, in 2023, we decided to shoot an actual documentary complete with a paranormal investigation, just like we did outdoors at Sandy Hook and Hudson Springs. Maybe the ghosts, if there were any, could steer us in the right direction.

With each visit not finding anything exciting, I am still drawn to this road as are countless others. For young people, it is simply a rite of passage if you live in the Bayshore area. It also attracts outsiders from all over the state on a nightly basis hoping to experience something creepy. On any given night, especially in October, you may find yourself in a bit of a traffic jam as people wind their way down this sometimes narrow and always bumpy dirt road.

It no doubt has the appearance of a place that might be haunted, or somewhere that someone might look to commit murder and dump a body. The thick forests that surround it give cover and can have a claustrophobic effect. This is worse in the summer when the leaves and branches are much thicker. In the fall and winter, as it starts to take on a more dead appearance, the setting becomes one where you could stage a horror movie.

But did anything dark truly happen on this road? Maybe something minuscule which blossomed into the outrageous? Unfortunately, Whipporwill Road may just be a complete invention, but one that did not have harmful intentions at first.

As we take our drive down, entering off Chapel Hill Road, the land dips and makes it seem that you are literally entering the pit of hell. Though usually referred to just as "Whipporwill," the full name of the road is technically "Whipporwill Valley." There was once a normal street sign that stood at this entranceway. It went missing a couple of years ago and was never replaced. Maybe it was taken as a souvenir by a visitor, or removed by locals who live along the road in an attempt to divert and confuse the nightly parade of the curious.

When you visit during the day, you can take in the foliage and natural beauty, and spot some multi-million-dollar mansions nestled in the woods that surround the road. Horse farms can be seen in various clearings. Some of the property was once owned by Armory Haskell, who served as vice president of exports at General Motors before founding his own successful glass company. He would become an avid sportsman, getting involved in horse-racing. He died in 1966, with the Haskell Invitational being held annually in his honor.

I recommend making your first visit in daylight so you can get a clearer picture of the atmosphere. When you return at night, you may have a calmer sense of where you are. Even as I gradually came to terms with none of the legends being true, driving on such an isolated road littered with holes and bumps—and, in some cases, the edges of the road crumbling into gutter-like crevices—can make for a scary ride, made infinitely more unnerving by thinking about how long it might take a tow-truck to find you in case you break down. Already on edge, as the darkness surrounds your vehicle and even the brightest moon struggles to beam through the trees, many ghostly legends begin to rear their heads and you will be on the lookout for them regardless of their veracity.

Perhaps the oldest of the "Big Three" stories involves the execution of witches in the 1800s who were burned to death and then buried under the road. This was done after they put a curse on the local farmers who served as their executioners. Legends say that as you drive down, you can count fifteen bumps, one for each witch. But the problems with this story are like the bumps themselves: too many to count. The timeline being the nineteenth century means that if someone, let alone fifteen people, were executed, it would be fact and not legend. It would appear in a newspaper or someone's diary, and we would not be wondering about the details, of which there are none. Witch-hunting and accusations of witchcraft were passé for well over a century by then.

Of all the legends discussed in this book and those to come, this is probably the laziest creation. Had it been set in the 1600s, it at least could have been considered that, before our area's population grew, maybe there were some kind of unholy practices occurring in colonial Middletown which needed to be stopped by those in charge. It also would have helped if the victims were hanged, which was the method of executing witches in North America, as opposed to burning. And had they been burned, it is likely their graves would not have caused much of a bump when dug. The witches, it would appear, are nothing more than an effective campfire tale.

Unlike Neidlinger's spies and Mandeville's pirates, there is no traceable source for stories of witches in Middletown or the Bayshore as a whole. There was no witch trial in the immediate area, of which rumblings or gossip could have spiraled out of control from. The colony, and later state, of New Jersey only had one recorded legal case involving a witch, and it was not actually a true witch trial. In 1727, Abigail Sharp of Woodbridge sued Abraham Shotwell for £500 because she claimed to have suffered social and financial damages after he claimed she was a witch. Shotwell had publicly accused her of transforming into a black cat, prancing on the roof of his house, and using supernatural powers to kill his horse. The court may have been so incredulous at the mere thought of this situation that they did not formally accuse Sharp of witchcraft and instead heard her arguments against his defamation of character. The verdict of the hearing has unfortunately been lost to time.

The same lack of origin also affects the legitimacy of Whipporwill's second major legend, which is devil worship. For any fringe group looking to practice rituals, the isolation of Whipporwill would seem to provide ample cover. Satanists and devil-worshipers have long been associated with conducting ceremonies and sacrifices in the thick forest that lines the road. However, like the witches, these older stories appear to be set in the 1800s. While people have worshiped the devil throughout history, the popularity and novelty of such practice was not mainstream until the 1960s when Anton LaVey created the Church of Satan in California. This would lead to the so-called "Satanic Panic" of the 1980s and '90s when Christian and moral figures across the country alleged that the devil was infiltrating unsuspecting minds and wreaking all kinds of evil havoc. One of the main causes of this submission to Satan was listening to heavy metal music.

This is not to say that no one has ever done anything ritualistic at Whipporwill. Remains of amateurish ceremonies and occult practices including dead animals, candles, and pentagrams can be found throughout the year. In our most recent visit to film the documentary for Ghosts on the Coast, we captured on camera a childish pentagram carved into a tree. I would say that most concerns people have about any rituals going on there should be put to rest. Teenagers playing around are not going to conjure up the devil himself, but Whipporwill would be the place to try, given the witchcraft connections and isolation. But then it must be considered that, depending on the time of year, it would be difficult to do anything extensive on the road or pulled over to the side.

As for the woods that surround the road, it is impossible to legally investigate further. On almost every other tree, on both sides of the road, from beginning to end, there are "No Trespassing" signs. In cases where you can see people's houses, the properties themselves would not be scary or alluring enough. But that thick forest where no traces of life or houses can be seen? It would be tempting to go for a walk. We have always had a rule that we would not ever do anything illegal to get footage, though the likelihood of being caught is slim. There are videos taken by explorers of abandoned places on YouTube who are anonymous that have ventured into these woods. Aside from some concrete structures and an old swimming pool that once belonged to the Haskell family, there does not appear to be anything too exciting. I guess the thrill of the chase outweighs the result.

There was a time when venturing off the road was not only allowed but encouraged at special events held by the Haskell family. His property on Whipporwill, now owned by someone else and forbidden to be explored, was known as Woodland Farms. This was the site of many "Haskell Hunts," which started in 1932 and lasted until Armory's death in 1966. Every year, friends and associates would be invited to enjoy the age-old aristocratic tradition of the fox hunt. This was combined with several horse races throughout the day while the invitees would enjoy champagne and *hors d'oeuvres* while dressed in their best and dining on fine linen tablecloths adorned with candelabras and decorations.

Could this be where whispers of clandestine activity began? While the Haskell Hunts are well-known and appeared to be nothing more than harmless fun, maybe it was outsiders who saw this annual meeting of the wealthy as something more. I do not believe anything inappropriate was happening there, but it is like grasping at straws trying to ascertain where such a legend might have been born. Meetings of Satanists, at least in popular culture, usually happen at a secluded mansion, attended by wealthy friends of the owner from far and wide, and have an air of luxury surrounding them. This might be where stories began. It could have been in hindsight during the "Panic."

The home in question on the property off the road was built in 1925. There were thirty-three interior designers and nine landscapers hired to complete the project. The house included a glass-walled solarium, upholstered furniture with hand-painted silk, and a carved solid oak billiard table on the third floor. The home was set on 700 acres of woods and farmlands. Armory lived there until the end of his life and is buried on the property in the Haskell's Cemetery plot. Unfortunately, in July 1966, less than three months after his death, the vacant home was set ablaze and destroyed by suspected arsonists. Over 200 firefighters battled the fire in the early morning hours, but it was to no avail. The smoke billowed over the property and could be seen as far away as Long Branch.

Following his death and subsequent fire, the hunt would continue but in a more informal way. Locals would be allowed to attend and pay to park their cars and tailgate. Money collected was donated to charity. There are newspaper clippings regarding these newer public hunts, with everyone seen having a good time. In fact, there do not appear to be any newspaper articles at all regarding anything suspicious at Whipporwill Valley Road until the 2000s, when they begin quoting stories that blossomed on the early days of the internet, and not the other way around as one might think. They have also popped up in issues of *Weird N.J.* over the years, but only along the lines of what is debunked here. The exceptions to this are a couple of accidental deaths and the disposal of a murder victim, which will be discussed later in the chapter.

As for the third major legend, could the woods by the road have been used as a meeting place for the Ku Klux Klan? This one can be labeled as plausible. It is a dark part of New Jersey history, but the Klan was highly active in Monmouth County during the 1920s. Beginning in 1923, the Klan experienced a resurgence and attempted to gain a stronghold in New Jersey. They rallied in Perth Amboy before being kicked out by angry residents who rioted at the thought of their presence. Looking for new stomping grounds, they were welcomed to the Jersey Shore by anti-liquor white protestants who felt that local and state law enforcement agencies were not doing enough to combat the various mafia groups, gangs, and bootleggers during Prohibition, some of which were aided and abetted by crooked politicians and policemen. They started with a cross burning and parade in Point Pleasant before working their way up the coast and quickly gaining traction in the Bayshore.

The Klan was adaptable based on their audience, and billed themselves as crusaders for Prohibition, making themselves more appealing to a wider range of people. Since immigrant gangs, mainly the mafia, were chief proponents in keeping liquor flowing freely on the Jersey Shore, they also became a prime target of the anti-immigrant, anti-Catholic Ku Klux Klan. They associated alcohol with the destruction of pure white America, and immigrants with bringing in the alcohol.

Nearby Atlantic Highlands was considered by many to be the capital of rum-running on the east coast of the United States. The Klan made their presence known. They got involved with stealing local elections and attempting to oust pro-liquor politicians. There is documented proof of the Klan rallying and causing violence in Middletown, Atlantic Highlands, Port Monmouth, and Red Bank, but nothing specifically ties them to Whipporwill Road, though, like the Satanists, it would be the perfect place to seek solitude.

It is also not necessarily true that the Klan would have needed to meet in secret at all, as their public rallies were well-attended by locals and New Jersey membership in their group swelled to an estimated 60,000–100,000 by 1925. The group would begin to falter in New Jersey as they became split over who their main targets should be— African Americans, Jews, and Catholics like the good old days or corrupt politicians, crime syndicate leaders, and bootleggers, which was the reason why they were invited here in the first place.

The Klan's rumored association with the road also leads to another popular legend, as many people have told tales of being chased away by groups of hooded Klansmen or by an angry old man in a red pickup truck, who could possibly be a Klansman himself. When finally posting our documentary, we were met with so many comments from people who had driven down the road over the years. It proved to be a nostalgic memory for many, as they recalled their childhood and taking that legendary journey along Whipporwill. More comments referenced stories of the Klan than anything else, though all were vague retellings of the familiar. The stories of being driven off the road are not stuck in time but continue to be professed to this very day.

While I could probably see a resident who lives along the road getting annoyed enough that they might want to chase an onlooker off their property, or playful enough to pull a prank, no one has ever managed to snap a photo or take a video of the actual chasing. A large group of Klansmen can be ruled out (I hope) in this day and age but, considering everyone that drives this road now is usually with a group of people in the vehicle, all of whom are filming or taking pictures, there should be some kind of evidence. There is none.

As for murders, unfortunately, the more recent history of Whipporwill does contain one ghastly story that is indeed true. On March 6, 1982, the body of twenty-two-year-old Nancy Clark of Fair Haven was discovered at the edge of the road near the paved area toward Chapel Hill with a single stab wound to her chest. She had last been seen at a bar in Sea Bright the previous night, getting into a white car with three men as she attempted to hitchhike home. According to police reports, she was taken to Scenic Drive in Atlantic Highlands, stabbed with a military-type knife in her heart, and driven to Whipporwill where her body was discarded. The police would go on to arrest two of the men involved, with Thomas W. Bailiff of Leonardo found guilty of the murder and sentenced to life in prison. He was released on parole in 2017.

There have also been two other deaths to occur on Whipporwill Road or a neighboring property, but both are well-documented, accidental, and not ruled as suspicious. The first was in 1989, when a Middletown Public Works employee was found dead in his truck on the road, victim of a suspected heart attack. Then, in 2006, a caretaker on one of the private properties located along the road also suffered a heart attack while riding his tractor. The police were called when someone spotted the tractor sticking out of an in-ground swimming pool. He apparently had the coronary episode, and while still seated on the tractor, it continued moving before falling into the pool. It took several officers to remove him, but they were too late. It was two days before Christmas, and the water was said to be near freezing. There are some articles online dealing with the creepy history of Whipporwill that will reference these deaths and also mention something along the lines of "there are rumored to be more," but, in reality, there are not, except for a few traffic accidents, none of which were fatal.

We set out on our paranormal investigation of the road already knowing full well that there were no witches, Satanists, or Klansmen, but we still wanted to see if anything was haunting this road. As we have experienced, sometimes you can be taken by surprise when you least expect it. In some cases, we phrased our questions to see not only if anything haunts the road, but if the ghosts themselves are aware of any of the outlandish stories. From a contact point of view, we were not looking for anything sinister to come through, but maybe the spirits of past workers on any of the surrounding farms and properties, or past travelers who remain stuck on the road.

A random spot was chosen to park our cars, since one place seemed to be as good as the next. The investigation got off to a strong start when I began by asking if there was anyone with us. We were immediately given the names "Smith," "Steve," and "Zach" through the SB-7, which we had hooked up with a larger speaker for better sound because of how open it was outside and also the wind that was blowing. Sometimes we go through entire investigations without getting a single name. When Patty asked how many spirits were with us, the response was "four." As she continued to ask questions, one voice said, "hate her," which we did not pick up in the moment, and then another "her" a few seconds later. Were they talking about Patty, the only female present, or just having a conversation amongst themselves? Other words and phrases were picked up, but they did not pertain to what we were saying.

As Patrick walked away from us toward a stone wall, two direct phrases were spoken to us, "Get out here," and as I began walking towards him, "Come back." Both of these we heard originally without needing further analysis. As Patrick and I were confirming this with each other, the same voice said "come back" yet again. At this point, Christian arrived in his car to the investigation, and as soon as he walked over, we heard a slow, "How are you?" and then his name, "Christian," shortly after that. I asked, "Who are you?" and a female responded emphatically, "No!" Christian then heard his name called a second time.

There was back and forth chatter on the other side, followed by two strong utterances of profanity that may or may not have been directed at us. It was so loud and clear that you can see us all reacting in the video with laughter as it took us by complete surprise. A third one was about to come a few seconds later. When the witches were brought up, that was met with "They're lying" and "What's that?" Asking about who, if anyone, drives a red pickup truck, the answer was a simple "him."

Before we began walking down the road with the SB-7 still scanning, Patrick asked if the spirits could tell us where the body of Nancy Clark was disposed of. A young female voice said, "Hi," an older female said, "pretty," and then when Patty cuts in and asks us if we heard anyone say "pretty," a man's voice answers her with "yes." We had way more intelligent responses at this point in the investigation than I ever thought we would. These were not abstract or fragmented bits and pieces of convenience that would hopefully fit our questions in hindsight, but clearly intelligent spirit responses that we were understanding in the moment, and apparent conversations between themselves in their world.

We continued walking down the road. Patrick walked backwards to film Christian and I, while Patty trailed behind with her tape recorder and headphones hoping to capture EVPs that were not coming through the Spirit Box. A voice told us to "find em," and then when we stopped walking, because we noticed a couple of town vehicles up ahead, something else said "don't." We ended up talking to one of the workers, asking him if he had personally ever seen or heard of anything strange happening on Whipporwill. He said other than a car accident last year, he had not.

Near where we had stopped to talk to the worker, who had now driven away, we turned off the SB-7 because we heard knocking noises coming from the woods. There were a few loud wooden bangs, and then a few that were not as loud. It was hard to determine what these sounds were. We could not see anything moving, and they were loud enough that they were not simply acorns or branches falling and making a tapping sound. This ended up being edited out of the documentary because we did not want to seem crazy with people thinking we had now stopped to talk to trees, asking them to "do it again."

Our group then headed back towards our cars, where we would hear a few more responses. One said "lead" and another "Don't … see her." Then came "tempting" followed by "Ansley." None of this made any sense, and so I figured I would bring up the legends of devil worship. I asked, "Why do people do rituals here?" and the answer was surprisingly, "a cult." I then asked if there are any Satanists, and we heard "probably."

We wound down the investigation and hit them with as many questions as we could, asking for the final word on witches, Satanists, and Klansmen. For the first time that afternoon, there were extended periods of radio silence. I think we had exhausted them, and they were simply done for the day. At the time and looking back, this was one of the more fruitful outdoor SB-7 sessions we had ever conducted. While we got some names, there is no telling who exactly we were speaking with. Aside from that strange knocking sound, which probably was not paranormal, we did not see anything strange. The amateurish pentagram carved into a tree was not properly drawn, done on too much of an angle.

There were no ghostly figures following us, though those are usually seen or imagined at night. We did not notice any K-2 or EMF spikes either. Whoever was talking to us might have kept at a distance. We received some comments after we posted the video that we should have done this investigation at night. While it would have been creepier, we wanted to show people what the road looked like in broad daylight. For much of it, especially in the beginning, we had overcast skies that threatened rain which never came. To me, this further helps to show the isolation in some areas, because you can see a deep nothingness when looking into the woods. We wanted to be able to walk around without having to worry about tripping, or impeding other cars, on top of closely paying attention to the SB-7 radio. We had also shot videos there at night in the past, and with our camera and flash capabilities, they never came out looking great.

The question that inevitably must be asked now is, "Where did all of these stories come from?" With the exception of the Klan having local involvement, everything else seems to be made up from thin air. One of the emails I received after the documentary was shared was by someone who said they had the answer as to why these three major legends dominated the history and pop culture of Whipporwill Road. It was a simple one, in that they were started by residents who lived along the road decades ago in an attempt to scare visitors and keep people from not only wandering around the surrounding woods, but from driving down it entirely.

I was also told this was the reason why the road has never been paved. It is not for lack of funding in the public works department, but to make it more difficult for normal travelers to drive down and to make them think twice about wanting to use it as a shortcut or see what it looks like. This notion then backfired, when all of these rumors and myths had the opposite effect: they did not keep people away, but instead made them more curious. As for the non-paving of the road, that too is believable. Neither can be confirmed but take a moment to imagine if it was paved. More drivers may use it out of convenience, but would it still draw the thrill-seekers?

Following the investigation, we drove to nearby Cooper Road which is usually a stop for most people either before or after Whipporwill. It is not entirely a dirt road, but there are some areas that look nearly identical and offer the same feelings of loneliness. My first drive down there years ago with Brett was in the summer, and I distinctly remember seeing the thick trees almost curve and hang over the road, making it seem like a tunnel. After a certain distance, cars will come across a bridge, which is an unexciting concrete slab with some steel railings over a narrow creek. This is called "Crybaby Bridge."

There are different versions of what happens here. Depending on who you ask, the legend states that the bridge is haunted by the ghost of an infant who either fell off or was thrown off of it and left to drown. If you park on it at night and lower your windows, you might be able to hear the faint sound of a baby crying, hence the nickname of the bridge. Another version says if you shut your car off in neutral, a strange force will push you across. Then there is a more frightening iteration: no force will push you, but when you turn the car back on, it will stall out and you will remain trapped on the bridge. No one confidently says what happens after the car has been rendered useless: do you simply call for a tow truck or does the spirit of the crying baby rise from the water and kill you?

When filming, Patty herself had yet another version of the tale, telling us that she had heard growing up of a local married couple in which the wife cheated on her husband, became pregnant, died in childbirth, and that the husband was so irate he murdered the baby by throwing him off the bridge. Nevertheless, on this particular day and several other late nights previously, we have yet to hear the elusive sounds emanating from "Crybaby Bridge."

In the end, it does not really matter what people such as myself have to say about whether the legends are true or false, because people just love to be scared. That is perfectly fine. Visitors should still drive down the road at night and try to have any thrilling experience that they can, because while there is the extreme likelihood nothing that will happen, it is still an activity that has been enjoyed for generations. My debunking of this should not affect anyone's fun, and I myself will assuredly drive down this road again in the future.

Take that drive. Count the witches' bumps. Look out for the Klansmen and the Satanists. Try to imagine the shadows of the trees dancing and coming to life like so many others claim they saw. Just make sure you have a full tank of gas, and that somebody in your party has AAA just in case. And should a red pickup truck appear behind you, try to remain calm—they are probably just as scared as you are.

Despite containing several private residences, farms, and barns, Whipporwill maintains an isolated feeling throughout most of the drive.

While it makes for a good story, and Whipporwill is the perfect setting, it is unlikely that such a scene ever played out, except in people's minds. (*London: T. Norris*)

A pentagram we found carved into a tree during our investigation of Whipporwill Road. (*Ghosts on the Coast/Patrick Osborn*)

THE DEFENDER OF THE 18TH AMENDMENT

The Ku Klux Klan are probably the last people that anyone was expecting to show up in a book about legends and hauntings, but aside from a racist ideology, they were also in favor of Prohibition. This led them to gain a stronghold in the Jersey Bayshore. (*Branford Clark*)

Armory Haskell, of horseracing fame, who owned property along Whipporwill Road where the "Haskell Hunts," became popular for decades. (*Monmouth Park*)

A Spirit Box session on Whipporwill Road. (*Ghosts on the Coast/Patrick Osborn*)

According to the legend, it was in this water which flows under "Crybaby Bridge" on Cooper Road that a child was murdered by his father. (*Ghosts on the Coast/Patrick Osborn*)

7

# THE GODFATHER'S GARDEN

## DEEP CUT GARDENS, MIDDLETOWN

By late 2022 heading into 2023, I had spent so much time at Deep Cut Gardens due to a monthly lecture series I was giving on Prohibition-era mobsters on the Jersey Shore that I began to wonder if the property or visitors' center was haunted. I did not have any experiences myself, and though I have known several people with intimate knowledge of the garden for many years, had not heard any stories of paranormal activity from them either. There is only one known "rumor" that has persisted, which I will address later in this chapter, but it is of the earthly variety. By spring of that year, in keeping with our group's new theme of investigating outdoor and unsuspecting places, I began sifting through my lecture research and combining it with new information about the property's former owner, mafia boss Vito Genovese, who figures prominently in my program.

When we released the video to our YouTube, I asked Patrick to include a disclaimer, something we had never done or felt the need to do ever before. I thought that because I was giving lectures for the park, I did not want it to seem that anyone tipped me off regarding ghostly activity, and that was the truth. Not only were there no known ghost stories, but asking workers who have been there late at night and by themselves churned up nothing creepy or unexplainable. We would be going into this investigation cold.

A few days after the video came out, I received a rather lengthy and nasty comment. It began by saying we were "full of it" (the original language was more colorful). At first glance, I thought, "Here we go. Someone thinks we are claiming this place to be haunted and did not bother to read the disclaimer or watch the end of the video when I give my closing thoughts." Instead, the person was angry that we said Deep Cut Gardens was likely not haunted. They claimed to be a long-time former employee who spent more than two decades working there and not only had numerous paranormal encounters themselves but said the place was "well documented as a haunted site."

Whatever this person's experiences were, they were never revealed. As for other activities being documented, I do not view that statement as plausible for the simple fact that nothing exists anywhere (except our video) tying the property to ghostly activity, or going so far as to ask the question and trying to find out. While Genovese was surely an infamous figure, that did not necessarily mean that anyone was hanging around in the afterlife. It was the first time in my career that someone was ever mad at me for saying a place was not haunted when it is usually the other way around. But still, I wanted to see for myself, as being the first to investigate an area has been fruitful in the past.

Whether any spiritual presence remains at Deep Cut is not even central to this chapter, though we did end up communicating with something during the investigation. The land is home to one of the most beautiful gardens in the state of New Jersey. Without any previous knowledge before arrival, you may scoff at the idea of anything dark or morbid being associated with it.

For nearly a century, both private owners and members of the public have marveled at Deep Cut's enchanting nature. But there is a dark side to this horticultural wonder, as it was built by mafia boss Vito Genovese, a cold-blooded killer who rose to prominence during Prohibition, and used this property as a retreat to escape the chaos at his other residences. He served as a partial inspiration for Mario Puzo's 1969 best-selling novel *The Godfather*, which was later turned into one of the most influential films of all time. But Vito's life and involvement in Middletown and the Bayshore area is probably more sinister than any ghosts.

Vito arrived in New York City in 1913 when he was fifteen years old and emigrated from Italy with his family. Like many young immigrant children at the time, he got involved with local gangs and petty crime. The family would soon move to Atlantic Highlands; by then, Vito had been inducted into the mafia at age eighteen. He was the first member of his family to do so and a choice that he alone made for himself. With connections in both the City and Jersey Shore, Vito quickly became a trusted and efficient gangster and mob enforcer. He got his start working for Arnold "The Brain" Rothstein and with a veritable gangster dream team of Lucky Luciano, Bugsy Siegel, and Albert Anastasia.

Between 1917 and 1930, he was arrested no less than eight times, for charges ranging from gun possession and burglary to counterfeiting and even homicide. His full arrest record is incomplete, with some parts simply missing over time. The charges were dropped in every instance. While Vito made his early fortune running prostitution rings in New York, he would begin his meteoric rise to power during Prohibition. His access to Atlantic Highlands, which was considered the rum-running capital of the east coast, contributed to this success. He became friends and associates with local gangster Andy Richard, who essentially ran the town. Richard might be one of the most interesting and powerful figures in Bayshore Prohibition history whose practically unknown story will be profiled in the next chapter.

Like many mob bosses throughout history, Vito had two sides: ruthless cold-blooded killer and kind man of the people who was loved by his neighbors. Genovese and Richard, among others in Atlantic Highlands, regularly attended mass at St. Agnes, were generous donors, good tippers in restaurants and businesses, and would do anything for a friend. The front steps of the church were paid for by Genovese himself. In speaking with someone who works for the parish, they recalled hearing a story that when it came time for the stone to be delivered, the workers were on strike for some unrelated issue. Vito made a couple of calls, and the stone arrived within a few days.

New Jersey and our popular culture has long been fascinated and obsessed with mafia figures. It has contributed to the popularity of movies and TV shows such as *The Godfather* trilogy and *The Sopranos*, the latter of which is set in New Jersey. Without Genovese, such projects may have never existed or commanded a strong enough market in which they could blossom. The split personalities of the bosses has always been evident, and Vito was a prime example. Regular people in town, who played no part in gangs or illicit activity, simply loved the guy. Upon posting our video to some of the local town Facebook pages, we were inundated with stories of people whose parents knew Vito or they themselves knew or worked for him as children.

There was not one negative comment to be found. Stories ranged from Vito tipping someone's grandfather a dollar on a 10-cent haircut to being overly generous with buying Girl Scout cookies from a local troop. He frequently paid children for odd jobs around his property, such as raking leaves or collecting tree branches that had fallen. He was also, apparently, a good cook.

However, when it came to business, or if someone crossed him, he was quick to act. He had a cold, icy stare which was partially hidden under thick tinted glasses. It was said he literally would not blink when ordering a murder. Joseph Valachi, a former member of the Genovese crime family, testified, "If you went to Vito and told him about some guy who was doing wrong, he would have this guy killed and then he would have you killed for telling on the guy." Such a mindset should surprise no one.

When I give my lectures on Vito, and now write this chapter, I hope to convey to people that I try my best to neither glorify nor vilify him, but simply state the facts. There are people who will always be enamored with such a lifestyle which has been romanticized for decades. The true nature of some of these mobsters, not just Vito, but his initial bosses, his friends, and cohorts, is one of extreme violence and we sometimes lose that human element as we become desensitized through various books, movies, and television shows. The Bayshore was an eyewitness to this frenzy of murder and power.

By 1935, Prohibition had been over for two years. Some mobsters attempted to legitimize their previous black-market businesses and others quit the game entirely. However, there was one more line of work that was about to blossom: the heroin trade. In the coming decades, Vito would help expand it internationally, but not before being named in several high-profile murders, including that of Ferdinand Boccia, and purchasing a 40-acre property in Middletown. This was known as the Dangler Mansion and Estate, which was constructed in 1925. The house was a ten-room Colonial Revival mansion that contained a separate gardener's cottage. Vito would buy the secluded property in 1935 to put more distance between himself and his business dealings. He immediately began making changes and expanded the house to twelve rooms, refurbished it with every modern convenience available, including building a new kitchen, and hired landscape architect Theodore Stoudt and the Caruso Construction Company of Atlantic Highlands to turn the sweeping land into an Italian villa.

Under direction from Genovese, Stoudt added a rockery and ponds, greenhouse, rose parterre, pergola, and a stone swimming pool at the edge of the property. In fact, the pool is probably in the most inconvenient place in the whole garden. It is not up on the terrace which overlooks the beautiful acreage but is instead all the way at the bottom, and quite a distance from the house. One of my many contacts alleged that Vito intentionally wanted the pool as far away as possible to keep prying eyes (including those of his wife) from seeing what he and his guests were doing. Just take a walk from that pool up the hill back to the house, and when you are done panting, you might see that as the best explanation.

A peanut-stone replica of Mount Vesuvius served as the exclamation point to this extensive project. The volcano was not only decorative but had a tinderbox underneath and worked as a fire pit. Deep Cut is situated at a high elevation on Red Hill Road. While it may seem far enough inland, the waters of the bay are only less than 5 miles away. This has led some to speculate that the volcano may have been used to send smoke signals. The tree line would have also been much lower in the 1930s, making it possible to have seen the bay with the help of a telescope or binoculars, lending some credence to this theory.

Vito became a U.S. citizen in 1936 and lived there until 1937 when he then fled the United States for Italy, with over a million dollars in a suitcase, which was packed by his wife, Anna, to avoid the murder charges from three years earlier. It was during his time away that the original mansion at Deep Cut burned down. According to some sources, his wife had visited the day before the fire to retrieve documents. The blaze was attributed to a faulty heating system and has remained suspicious ever since.

While in Italy, Vito worked for Benito Mussolini before switching over to the United States Army at the end of World War II, where he acted as an interpreter. He used this access to the army to steal goods and re-route trucks, selling the items at high prices to desperate war-weary Italians. Anna visited him regularly in Italy and while he told her how much he loved her, he cheated on her with prostitutes several times. This was his second wife; the first had died in 1931 and their marriage had been violent and tumultuous. Vito was physically abusive to the first wife, also named Anna. As she lay on her deathbed stricken with tuberculosis, Vito was not at her side, something which she was grateful for. She confided that he was a monster and that she was glad to finally be away from him. His second marriage, while not filled with physical abuse, was not much better.

Vito was back in the United States by 1945 and was immediately charged with the very murder he fled for. The case was eventually dismissed due to lack of evidence—and living witnesses. He and Anna would sell the Deep Cut estate in 1948 and move back to Atlantic Highlands, into a nearly million-dollar mansion on Ocean Boulevard where they would live lavishly. This house still stands today as a private residence, but it has been remodeled so much since Genovese owned it that it bears hardly any resemblance at all. His business partner and builder Dominic Caruso was the buyer, who sold the land to Karl and Marjory Whitol in 1952. The current house that stands today was built two years later.

By now, Anna had previously sued Vito for maintenance (which was alimony of the day) and later sought divorce. She told the judge, "All I want is three hundred and fifty dollars a week, but I want you to know my husband is a millionaire many times over." While Vito had allowed her to have anything she wanted, he was still cruel and a difficult man to live with. She would win her case, and though dropped the divorce, used the proceedings as a chance to sound off on the mafia underworld. She publicly told of Vito's illegal dealings and is credited with being the first mafia wife to shed light on a world that few members of the public had ever been allowed to see. For years people have wondered how she herself managed to stay alive. I met another local historian at one of my lectures who does presentations solely on Anna Genovese. He told me that she would end up receiving protection from Luciano for the rest of her life.

Anna herself lived quite a colorful life of her own both while with Vito and after. While he was in exile, she used some of the family's considerable wealth to open a series of nightclubs and bars in New York City, and she became one of the earliest open LGBT allies, where such customers could patronize her bars free of trouble and persecution. For this, she came under scrutiny from law enforcement, but she never backed down. For the 1930s and '40s, such behavior was remarkable.

Following the separation, Vito lived modestly at a small home in Atlantic Highlands on West Highland Avenue that looks almost identical today as it did back then. He rented it from his good friend Andy Richard. By this time, he had accumulated several nicknames such as "The King of Crime," "King of the Rackets," and, most infamously, "The Boss of All Bosses."

Vito would be photographed and interviewed in the 1950s, and unintentionally built up the image of a lovable Godfather-type character. He was seen raking leaves, relaxing in a favorite chair, cooking pasta sauce, hanging out at his house having a cigarette, and just being normal. But he never lost his power, still ordering frequent hits and making a fortune off the heroin black market. The number of murders he was responsible for in his lifetime could be in the hundreds.

Vito's reign would finally come to an end in 1959 when he was sentenced to fifteen years in federal prison on narcotics charges. Many thought the case was trumped up, in an effort to finally put Vito behind bars for all the other murders and crimes he got away with, much like Al Capone getting nailed for tax evasion in Chicago. He would live another ten years, dying in prison in 1969.

His funeral mass was held at St. Agnes Church, but such a ceremony was not without protest. In his early life, he was a much-loved figure in town, with many ignorant (intentionally or sincerely unknowing) of his crime-related activities. By now, his notoriety was too much to turn a blind eye to. Many townspeople and parishioners were horrified at the thought of a murderer being laid to rest out of their church. Some say the mass was only done as a favor to Vito's daughter who was a teacher at the church's parochial school. Under those circumstances, the mass was to be a low-key affair with photographers kept outside.

Cary Vena, whose assistance was so vital to me in the Spy House chapter, approached me when she saw my series at Deep Cut advertised. She asked if she could come along to take pictures, and then dropped the little nugget of information that her mother (who is still alive as of publication of this book) was the organist at this mass. I figured this was an incredible opportunity to learn more information about what transpired. Carly said she would talk to her about it, and ended up telling me that her mother did not remember much—because she was only in second grade at the time. Unable to wrap my mind around why such a young child was tasked with playing the organ at this far-from-ordinary mass, she told me that they could not find any adult organists who would agree to play, and that as a last resort, they asked her mother's family if they could use their daughter. She must have had just enough musical knowledge and ability to get through the hymns.

Such controversy was not lost on Reverend Michael Lease who performed the mass. He did not once mention Vito by name, not in the eulogy or at any other time. He simply ended the sermon with, "Let us remember the deceased in our prayers." Vito's forty years in Monmouth County and fifty in a life of crime were over. His body was then carried out over the very steps his money helped install years earlier, before he was transported to New York for burial. Anna would join him in 1982, buried right beside Vito despite their public falling out.

In subsequent years, Deep Cut Gardens would once again thrive under the Whitol family who added a new swimming pool, which is now the lily pond, and restored the gardens and greenhouse. Half of the property was willed to the Monmouth County Park System in 1977 by Marjory Whitol with the stipulation that they would purchase the other half. It has been enjoyed for free by the general public ever since. Vito Genovese's legacy has not been forgotten either. The house which now serves as a horticultural center has panels where people can learn the history of the park and how he shaped what it is today.

Visitors do frequently ask about him when they see a park ranger or worker. The lecture series I have been allowed to give, now in its second year and already scheduling a third, also helps to give people the knowledge of Vito and his associates. People are amazed to learn all this history which happened right in their own backyard. The next chapter of this book will discuss some of the other Prohibition-era characters in Atlantic Highlands and neighboring towns, and may prove just as shocking.

The question inevitably asked at some point in my presentation is, "Are there any bodies buried on the property?" It is a forgivable assumption given how large the area is and with so many mob stereotypes fresh in people's minds. After one of my lectures in 2022, an older gentleman in attendance approached me when it was over. He said his father had worked for Vito, doing yard work as a child there, and was told by another worker to never dig by the woods near the old swimming pool, because of what might be buried there. I would like to think he was joking with me or maybe just spinning a yarn. Nevertheless, the answer to such a question is "Probably not."

Nothing has ever been found, but we cannot say so for sure. However, the fact that this is an active garden with frequent digging and excavations means if there was something buried, it likely would have been found already. Right around the time this guy approached me, there was an ongoing project extending a pathway headed towards that swimming pool area. Nothing was found. It would have been foolish of Vito, or any mobster, to bury the evidence of a murder on their own property. If there was anyone buried, it could have been by rivals who sought to dump a body there while he was in exile and the area was abandoned for extended amounts of time, figuring if anything was ever found, Vito would get the blame. That is as far as I would be willing to consider the possibility. But if I woke up one morning and saw the headline, "Human Remains Found at Deep Cut," would I be surprised? Absolutely not. This will forever be a popular myth and the most-asked question at the park in terms of its past.

We began our paranormal investigation of the property on an afternoon in March. The gardens were practically devoid of visitors. Unlike some other places we have investigated that have murky pasts or multiple uses, Deep Cut is extraordinarily well-documented, not just of Vito's time but others. This made asking questions through the SB-7 exceptionally easy. We knew exactly what to target. Whether or not we would get any answers was a different story. Would "The Godfather" himself be present? Like William Franklin and his association with the Proprietary House, Vito only spent around two years out of his life on the property, and that was part-time at most. Still, this was a place that he designed himself and is probably more beautiful than any other home he lived at. Perhaps he still walks the gardens, reminiscing about the old country.

The investigation started in a program room inside the visitors' center. Though this was not the original house, spirits tend to interact and communicate based on what they are seeing in their time. This makes investigating an empty field possible if a house once stood there, because it is believed that the ghosts might still be seeing the house as it once existed.

The very moment I turned the SB-7 on, there was a scream followed by the name "Alberta" and then "Matthew" a minute later. From then on, we were greeted with one full phrase after another, such as "Inside manner," "Let him come," and the longest yet, which was "You're the only possible…" before getting cut off. In between all this was a clear "gavel," which is fitting considering how much time in court Vito and his friends spent. Maybe they were trying to tell us about one of the murder cases. When I asked how many spirits there were, we received the same answer as both the Halyburton Memorial and Whipporwill Road, which was "four." That seemed to be the magic number on these investigations.

Right after telling us how many of them there were, we apparently listened in on a conversation between two female spirits with personality. These sentences had some attitude and inflection and were not just monotone as most responses are. One said to the other, "You do *what?*" as if surprised, and was answered back with, "Aren't cha?" Two seconds later, another female says, "Vito" and later, "A lot happened." A male voice then added, "Whatcha call it?" I do not think I was ever part of an investigation where we received more questions asked back to us or among themselves as we were trying to ask them.

At this point in the session, we realized that something special was going on. A male slowly intoned, "In the other house over," which was not in response to a question. He was clearly trying to steer us in the direction of the old gardener's cottage, which is just a short walk away and is original to the property. It has been used as storage and is currently undergoing renovations to be turned into another activities building. I started asking my next question right as that sentence was finishing up. I brought up the rumor about bodies being buried on the property. The next responses we got were fascinating. The same male that uttered the previous statement says, "All that this," and then two different voices add, in a fragmented fashion, "water" and "and there's one…" but unfortunately could not finish the sentence. In the back of our minds, we had the rumor of bodies being buried by the old swimming pool, which made sense in this context. However, the cottage is located right next to the newer pool added by the Whitol family. There were two ways we could continue.

It was tempting to move to another location, but we had the spirits talking right where we were. I bluntly asked where the bodies were buried, and we heard "ground." After a few more questions that did not garner answers, a man says, "monster." Was he talking about Vito, maybe one of his victims trying to reach out? Shortly after, we were told to "go away." I continued by asking if the spirits knew why Vito had to flee the United States in 1937, and a female voice snapped back with another long sentence, asking rudely, "Why are you questioning him?" to which a man responded, "Vito, like me…" and then "newspaper looking." There were now so many different voices coming through, and when I asked who we were talking to, a woman said, "Pick on me."

I persisted, asking to specifically know who we were talking to and to give us a name. A man said to this, "I would neva" in a pure wise-guy accent. It took a while for these amazing responses to sink in. Being present in the moment is like being on a hunt, trying to follow the pieces of a puzzle with clues leading you around. It takes time to realize just how rare it is to not only get full sentences, but ones that are relevant to the investigation. While one-word answers are fine and usable, and sometimes make sense, it is much more conclusive to get a string of words over many radio sweeps to rule out that we are not just mistaking noise for a single word. It is much harder to confuse a full sentence.

Our group moved into the library on the other side of the house. Before we could set the Spirit Box down, we heard "Vito" again, followed by an annoyed, "That's it. I'm fine. Leave." A minute later, "That's a kill," and when I asked where we should go next, there was a slow, "go … die." It appeared that they were getting tired of our presence after all. We then picked up on what we thought was another conversation on the other side, with one man saying, "You're a rat," and the other, "Let's go, man."

With that, we went over to the cottage. It was here that we would have our first K-2 spikes of the investigation. Since this building was original to the grounds, I was hoping that the outstanding communication between us would continue. We started out on friendlier terms than how we ended in the main house, with a male voice asking, "How can I help you?" There was then a remark to another presence in the house, "Right, Richie?" The K-2 meter then spiked and we heard, "I'm done" and "Henry?" as if it was a question.

Since this house is where Vito's servants and groundskeepers would have lived, I asked if anyone there worked for him. One answered, "friend," and shortly after, a lady said, "Back in the day…" When I asked what her name was, we heard "Anna" clear as day. Was Anna Genovese with us? Someone that worked for Anna? Or a different woman altogether? Soon after, I explained to the camera about this being the oldest building on the property, dating to the 1920s when the Danglers owned the land. At this moment, the K-2 meter lit all the way up to red, which is the highest energy level it can detect. There was definitely something with us in that room. Patrick aimed the camera down at the meter, which was still pulsating at yellow (the middle of the range), and a voice said, "Hey Greg," and another, "hello."

The conversation then took a weird turn, and the full sentences returned. "Is there any way out of here?" came first, followed by, "Your eyes are open," after I asked if Vito ordered any hits while living at Deep Cut. The answer was a cryptic, "Died out from age." We continued to get scattered words and phrases, but nothing as concrete as what we were hearing in the visitors' center. After a few more minutes, we moved outside to the volcano and then finished up at the pergola. Our questions were met with mostly silence, but as Patrick joked that Patty and Christian looked tired because they were sitting on a bench, we heard a voice say, "Pick them up." We ended the investigation shortly after.

For a place that does not have a single ghost story associated with it, we were blown away by the amount of intelligent responses and K-2 meter readings. There is no telling how much more we would have been able to uncover if we conducted more investigations. I did not want to push our luck by returning again and again. We were more than satisfied, from the full sentences to the questions thrown right back to us, and those couple of "wise guy" remarks.

To claim that Deep Cut Gardens is "haunted" is tricky, simply because workers have coexisted peacefully with any possible ghostly entities who have never made themselves known until we went looking for them. But when we started to prod, they came out in full force and ready to speak. They must enjoy having such a beautiful place to spend eternity, and there is assuredly nothing malicious walking the grounds. We do not think that Vito came through on this day, but whoever we spoke to definitely knew who he and Anna were, and such knowledge was good enough for us.

Deep Cut Gardens is open every single day of the year and has something for everyone. Whether you are interested in mob and Prohibition history, or just want to get lost in its beauty, I invite people to come and go for a stroll. In the summers, the park is sometimes open until 9 p.m. when the sun has set and for a little bit after. Following one of my nighttime lectures in August, I lingered on my walk back to the car. There were no visitors, nor were there any lights in the garden area. No noise to be heard except those of nature. It was a transcendent experience of pure peace and tranquility. Like the great Civil War battlefields which once saw so much bloodshed and horror but are now beautiful national parks full of wonder, the irony of this place being built by a mass murderer is almost unconscionable. Life constantly weaves the cruel with the serene, and there is no better example of that in the New Jersey Bayshore.

Vito Genovese, shortly before his 1959 conviction on narcotics charges. (*Library of Congress*)

Deep Cut Gardens when Vito Genovese owned the property. The original mansion, which he expanded, can be seen on the hill. This photograph was likely taken where the swimming pool would be constructed. (*Monmouth County Park System*)

A close-up view of the garden from Genovese's time. Not much has changed since, including the pergola, which still stands. (*Monmouth County Park System*)

A young Anna Genovese before her life would begin to change in ways that she probably never thought possible.

Vito's peanut stone replica of Mt. Vesuvius. The hole underneath is the tinderbox area where a fire could be lit, thus sending smoke out the top of the volcano.

The largest area of the garden, constructed in an Italianate style.

No detail was overlooked, including this specimen of Sargent's Weeping Hemlock, which overlooks the rockery and ponds.

8

# MOBSTERS AND MURDERS

## ST. AGNES THRIFT SHOP, MOTHER TERESA REGIONAL SCHOOL, ATLANTIC HOUSE RESTAURANT, AND SMODCASTLE CINEMAS, ATLANTIC HIGHLANDS

Vito Genovese may have been the big name in Atlantic Highlands, but it was Andy Richard who ran the town. I have worked and volunteered here in one form or another since 2011. In addition to my historical fieldwork with the town's historical society, I also taught and coached hockey and baseball at the same St. Agnes School where Vito's daughter worked (she was long-since retired and it had been renamed Mother Teresa Regional School by then) and I have also worked at several restaurants in town.

When you manage to be in so many different settings, networking and mingling with a wide array of people, it is easier to understand just how important Prohibition, and the following years where mobsters were still active, is to this town. This is not ancient history in some far away land, but less than a century ago right in our own backyards. I came to know countless people who knew the very characters I would end up lecturing about or had parents who had dealings with them.

Soon after I joined the Atlantic Highlands Historical Society in 2013, I immediately became fascinated with the local Prohibition history, of which I knew little of previously. It was my work with this organization, housed at the Strauss Mansion Museum (where this book will reach its finale in a couple of chapters) that I began to hear and collect stories. People frequently come to the museum with questions about their properties. The building houses an archive and library which includes table-sized tax maps from the turn of the twentieth century and it is possible for residents in Atlantic Highlands, Leonardo, and parts of Middletown to research their property and how it may have changed. There are also a lot of people who are new to town, who want to know the history of Atlantic Highlands and maybe see if they are now living in a home with any kind of notoriety or special owners over the years.

Then there are the stories of people who would reach out because they had strange "nooks and crannies" in their basements, and possibly tunnels underneath their homes. This was a theme that persisted when I first became active in the Atlantic Highlands history community to this very day. There are more people than I can count that have relayed stories of vast tunnel systems underneath the town, either from one building to another, or to the water of the bay where illegal booze was brought in and then transported underground to safety.

There cannot be any discussion of tunnels without bringing up Vito's friend Andy Richard, who truly was the man in charge in Atlantic Highlands. Like so many mobsters, he grew up with a pretty normal life. Most of these soon-to-be killers usually had run-of-the-mill lives and childhoods until they got involved in illegal activities. These were not people born into lineages of crime, but usually young men bored with the world looking to do something fun and make a boatload of money in the process. The earliest bootleggers (a term used interchangeably with rumrunners) were just that. At a time when the average person earned around $30 a week, it was possible to earn hundreds or thousands by simply driving around with a car full of booze. As Prohibition expanded and became more drastic, gangs and violence increased, and such a job was no longer fun and lucrative but extremely dangerous.

Atlantic Highlands was once the capital of rum-running on the entire east coast, in addition to being a destination resort town. It had close proximity to New York City, thousands of people arriving daily by steamer and train, the Central New Jersey Rail Line, and nearly seventy hotels and boarding houses in operation from the height of the Victorian era into Prohibition. Richard's backstory is murky, but he arrived in town around this time after owning a liquor store in Bayonne and finding himself without a profession. The opportunities to be had in the Bayshore area were no secret, and so he moved himself and his wife (who had a daughter from a previous marriage) to a house on Garfield Avenue.

Richard grew to be so powerful that he had the chief of police, John Snedecker, in his pocket. They worked in tandem along with others to ensure that on nights when major imports of illicit cargo were coming in to the piers, the power station would shut off for a couple of hours so that it might be unloaded under the cover of darkness. As the years went by, Snedecker needed more than just monetary payment to look the other way and began taking some of the cargo for himself. The bootleggers tried to have him killed, but Richard managed to stop it, not only to save his cohort but to prevent it from being a big mess that might blow their cover.

Out of all of the Prohibition characters to exist, I am more fascinated by Richard than any of them. This was someone who exerted so much influence and power (which continued after Prohibition) and yet he is barely known. While his name is either famous or infamous in town with old-school locals, many have never heard of him. There are entire books written about Prohibition in New Jersey that only mention him in brief passing or not at all. I heard stories of his tunnels and of murders he orchestrated, but would there be a way to prove any of it was true?

At one of my lectures at Deep Cut in 2022, I was approached by one of his granddaughters who is friends with Patty and was excited to be seeing the presentation because she thought it was mainly about Vito. She was rather stunned when I got to an entire section on her grandfather. Before the program, I told her that I had information about him but was not sure what was fact and what was mainly just lore. She said to just go ahead with what I had and that we would talk when I was done. Except for a few minor details, I ended up having most of it right. This was an interaction I would never forget, and one that was not without morbid humor as I had to speak about all the people this guy killed in front of his granddaughter. When it was over, she joked, "Hey, that's my granddaddy you're talking about!"

But she was a good sport and told me about how Vito was over the house many times for lunch or dinner, and no one thought anything of it; how he was always super nice to the children and made sure to greet them and have a chat. He and Andy would then talk business, and Andy frequently cooked for him. Like Vito, he was a good cook, with another one of his relatives who I met the next year telling me that he made a delicious turkey soup.

With Patty's help contacting a third relative, I was provided pictures of Andy and got to see him for the first time. This person gave me permission to use them in future talks. There are none online and none published in any book to my knowledge. So, there he was. I had lectured about him for five years up to this point and never knew what he looked like. And boy, did he ever look the part, though the pictures were taken when he was older than this time period. I was informed that somewhere along the line, there was one of him with Al Capone in Chicago, but the family could not locate it. She told me how nervous her grandfather was to meet him, since he was merely a little fish out there compared to his Bayshore home.

I had two major questions for her. Yes, there was the issue of the famed tunnels, but also details about the murder of his first wife. So, the story went, and managed to be true, while Andy was in hiding in Canada to evade charges for murder, he suspected his wife was being unfaithful to him (in the business sense, with another gang) and sent his brother, George, to kill her at their house on Garfield Avenue.

He knocked on the door and was greeted by the wife, his sister-in-law. He told her to get in the car, which is never something you want to hear from a gangster. This was confirmed by a couple of her friends who were there and witnessed the entire incident. She looked out the window and apparently did not like who she saw in the car and refused to get in. It was at this moment that George pulled out a gun, shot her once in the chest, and as she fell to the floor dead, he threw the gun down and exclaimed something to the effect of, "I don't know why I did that!" and ran out of the house. The car then floored it and drove on off down the street. Another vehicle pulled up slowly, as if checking out the scene, before following behind the other. It was said that Snedecker was inside this second car, making sure the deed was done.

When Andy returned from Canada and safely managed to find his charges dropped, he married his dead wife's daughter from her first marriage. According to the family, the stepdaughter was close in age to Andy (he was in his early thirties and she in her mid-twenties) and never quite got along with her mother. She was happy that her mother was done away with, and only requested one item from Andy, which was to move to a new house because she found the thought of living at a murder scene unsettling. They soon moved into a much nicer home that was owned by the recently deceased world-famous Shakespearean theater actor Robert Bruce Mantell. The property contained a large mansion and a barn where Mantell held rehearsals for his acting troupe. It had been named "Brucewood" after his middle name. The two lived happily ever after until his death some three decades later, with her being a loving, doting wife, mother, and grandmother.

One of the relatives told me of an incident one night at this house that took place years after Prohibition. She was a child and was staying there for the night. When she arrived, she noticed cars lined up and down the street. She entered the house and was told by her grandmother to just go upstairs to her room and no matter what she heard, to just stay there and keep quiet. There was unintelligible arguing for several hours, well into the night. The next morning, she went downstairs and saw a newspaper on the kitchen table. There was a picture of someone on one of the pages, the face of which had been stamped out by numerous cigarette butts. A few days later, this person ended up dead. That was what the argument was about, and such a scene would have been prevalent not just at Richard's home but all over the Bayshore as mobsters and gangs jockeyed for power during and after Prohibition.

This building is currently the St. Agnes Thrift Shop, after Richard later sold it to the neighboring church, which is next to the school. This house has its own share of ghost stories associated with it. It could be that so many people have had feelings of dread in different buildings on the property because of the negative energy emanating from past incidents which resulted in murder, even if such murders did not occur in that particular spot.

Andy owned and operated a liquor store and bar on First Avenue after Prohibition. When alcohol was still illegal, this same building was one of possibly hundreds of speakeasies in town. Following the ending of the ban on booze, it became a popular bar, Andy's Tavern, which was in operation for decades. By the 1970s, after changing hands several times, it was purchased by two new owners who turned it into one of the first dedicated barbecue restaurants in New Jersey, the Memphis Pig Out. It is now operating as The Atlantic House. This is where reverberations of the past would come back with force in Atlantic Highlands. Remnants of a tunnel were found bricked up by the owners of the Pig Out, as were cases of unopened liquor bottles that must have been forgotten there by Richard decades earlier.

People still talk about this discovery, and of tunnels which are seemingly all over town. As recently as the day that I began writing this chapter, another local historian posted in an Atlantic Highlands Facebook group asking if anyone had any information on these tunnels for a project he was working on. Hundreds of people responded, echoing mostly the same legends that have spread over the years. Most pointed to the Thrift Shop as the source, since it was large and Richard lived there for many years.

Having worked at the school, which is on the property, I had heard all these stories before and been there many times. There were also tales of the house being haunted, but not by Richard or his family, but by the Mantells who occupied it previously. Robert, who we will examine in the next chapter, died there in 1928, and his third wife passed away suddenly at age thirty-seven on Halloween night in 1911—that is not legend, but a perfectly spooky fact. Everyone from coworkers to students (some of whom volunteered at the shop) had some kind of story about a lady in a white dress walking the halls, and many saw her looking out from one of the windows, originally thinking it was just a worker before realizing the shop was closed. The third floor is said to be particularly active. Patrick, who worked there on and off for years, once thought he saw the tall shadow of a man darting down the hallway. Since this is church property, I would never think to ask to investigate, therefore we might never know for sure.

The property was owned by Thomas Henry Leonard, the founder of Atlantic Highlands. He sold it to his son, James, who had the house constructed in approximately 1865–1867. The style was considered to be more "conservative" for the time period, when most Victorian mansions were being built with dramatic architectural embellishments. He lived there for about thirty years, becoming a successful steamboat captain in town and later an assemblyman.

Farther down the line, the house was sold to a Civil War veteran who owned it for a little more than a decade before selling it to Mantell. The actor turned it into a summer home paradise where he could quietly rehearse his scripts. He would go on to add a third floor, increasing the mansion to seventeen rooms, a wrap-around porch, several barns, and designed fences and gardens for the property, making it more beautiful than it had ever looked before. This single house was owned by three different historic figures, two locally and one nationally. It is hard to find a place with such a rich, diverse ownership.

In terms of other tunnels, I had asked the manager of the shop, Roseanne Musone Tierney, if I could see the basement. I knew her from my days working at the school. The floor was cemented over at some point, and there was nothing noticeably strange about any of the walls. If there was one, it is long sealed. Then there is the possibility of the tunnel starting in the barn that was once on the property. It was situated where the school's gym and stage are. I asked both relatives what they thought of the possibility of tunnels. The first said she personally never saw one, but if there was one, it was likely from the Thrift Shop property to the house he owned on adjacent West Highland Avenue that he rented to Genovese.

The second said there definitely was a tunnel, but it was just a small shaft from the Genovese rental to a house close by, and it was mainly there for them to hide in to make it look like no one was home. Other rumors, both with unknown sources and from people I know personally, name the Fireman's Field House (now near a baseball field) as the destination where one or all of these tunnels ended. Another coworker from when I was at the school said the old house she grew up in on that same street had a door in the basement that her father had bricked up because he did not want them going behind it to play. Was that a tunnel too?

Hearing and reading what people had to say about these is fascinating, but is it possible for a vast tunnel system to still exist? It must be considered because of the sheer amount of booze coming in through this town, but with all the construction that has happened over the years, would one not have been found already? And if there are any, it is most likely they have been flooded after several damaging storms, most recently Hurricanes Irene and Sandy in 2011 and 2012. With the exception of the Memphis Pig Out, and another one documented on Center Ave where the Atlantic Highlands Catamaran Club is, all everyone has is stories without proof, making them legends that will likely stand the test of time as only that. Until a large system is found, that is all they will be. I hope the day comes where one is discovered, not only to serve as proof but to help with my own research on the time period and get people excited about history. If anyone in town reading this has an unexplainable door in their basement that they have always been afraid to open, please reach out to me.

There are several locations in this chapter as my research and life experiences have led me from one place to another. I worked at the school from 2011 until it closed in 2016. I had a share of paranormal experiences happen there, all in broad daylight. When I first started there as a hockey coach, and became a substitute teacher, followed by some long-term assignments and then teaching middle school history classes, I never gave any thought the school would be haunted. Since it has now been closed for seven years and will never reopen, I see no harm in sharing some of them.

By the time I worked there, our first YouTube Channel was developing and then came our switch to Ghosts on the Coast. It was a small school where everyone knew everybody, and it was impossible to keep the channel from being known. Some of the middle school students and their siblings had also volunteered at the Strauss Mansion Museum, which was openly haunted. I had just joined the board of directors there after leaving the Proprietary House.

The principal at the time called me into their office one day for a chat. After a few school-related matters, this person looked me in the eye and said, "I know the kids watch your YouTube and volunteer at the Strauss Mansion but please do not tell them this school is haunted." I leaned back, a bit stunned and said, "Is this school haunted?" The individual smiled and all they would say is that when working after dark, there were times they did not feel alone. That was a common theme from several teachers and staff. Most never saw anything but just felt like something was "off." Yet one told me of seeing shadows walking down the hallway, which was gloomily illuminated only by a red emergency exit light at night. I can honestly say that being on the upper floors at night with no lights on truly was terrifying and the perfect setting for the mind to play tricks on itself.

Like the Brookdale Campus, I never imagined the ghosts of any former students or teachers being there, but most likely the land's use before it was a school. This was before I knew anything other than the basics about Andy Richard, but I was aware of Robert Mantell. I surmised that if the Thrift Shop was haunted, the school, which is where his barn was located, might be too.

One afternoon as I was walking through the empty gym with the lights off to get something out of my car during a free period, I heard a basketball bouncing. It sounded like it was coming from the stage. It was only two or three bounces, like my presence startled it and then it dropped the ball and left. I walked over just in case, and there was nobody there. It might have been the next year that, while with a class on the third floor, a door unlatched itself, opened, and slammed shut. This was not a draft caused by an open window. Both myself and the entire class clearly heard the latch. They were taking a test and it was quiet. I looked up, expecting to see someone entering the room, but there was no one at the door. There was a child throwing something out in a garbage can by this door at the time, and they ran away when this happened. Everyone was looking at me, the ghost hunter, for an explanation. Unable to acknowledge it, I just shook my head and laughed.

Shortly before the time came to write this book, a former student reached out to me and discussed the possibility of having a small reunion with some of her classmates at the Strauss Mansion, where we had a field trip many years ago. She also said, "And then you can finally tell us that really scary ghost story that happened at the school." Nothing came to mind, and I asked her what she was talking about. Apparently, one day, I told her class that I had a really good ghost story and that I could only tell it to them after they graduated. I wracked my brain for days trying to figure out what she meant, and then came to the lackluster conclusion that I think I only promised them that so they would be quiet.

Never was any investigating equipment brought into the school out of respect for the kind of school it was, but it did not seem necessary. Students and coworkers constantly had experiences, mainly occurring after the school day ended when the quiet could take hold. Parents I met also steered me to other locations in town. Two of these would be the Memphis Pig Out, where one's child worked as a busser, and the Atlantic

Cinemas where another worked at the ticket booth. The theater has had two different iterations since: Atlantic Movie House and now SmodCastle Cinemas, which is owned by world-renowned director Kevin Smith.

I was told that at the Pig Out, there were constantly items being moved around, and people saw figures from the past. We never thought to ask to investigate there under past ownership; though, last year, the manager of the Atlantic House Restaurant did let us leave Patty's trap camera in the basement overnight to see if it would capture any spirit movement. Unfortunately, it did not, but they were open to a possible investigation in the future. But during the Pig Out years, one source told me that the main spirit haunting the joint was a lady named Eleanor "Ellie" Huson. She became a local celebrity of sorts, living to the ripe old age of 106 and partying and enjoying life right until the very end.

She was purported to be the restaurant's first ever customer and returned weekly, dining in the same chair at the same table for decades, until her death in 2009. When she turned 100, the town threw her a birthday party. By then, the restaurant not only made sure her table was ready for her, but had her name inscribed on the back of her chair. A contact who knew her told me that Ellie was fond of the Pig Out's barbecued chicken and always had a glass of sherry wine to drink with it. In her later years and being unable to drive, the owner would pick her up and bring her to dinner and then return her home.

Ellie was apparently a personality not to be missed. As a child, her father met with Theodore Roosevelt who gave her one of the original Steiff Company Teddy Bears. She was a raconteur with a love for life, and so many stories to be heard. Both the chair and stuffed animal are on display at the Strauss Mansion. We will never know if Ellie continues to dine at the Memphis Pig Out in the afterlife. A parent of a former student told me that when her children were little, they would point to an older lady sitting at one of the tables. Since the table was vacant, it was assumed they were seeing her spirit. We hope she is still enjoying herself and partying on the other side, though I would love to know what she thinks of the Atlantic House's renovations.

Spirits are and have been prominent in Atlantic Highlands, both the ghostly and drinking kind. Across the street is the movie theater, which operated for years as the Atlantic Cinemas. For as long as anyone can remember, there were rumors that the building was haunted. One of my student's siblings worked there and had stories of patrons complaining that they were being poked or touched while watching movies. Some had their legs grabbed from underneath their seats. Workers consistently heard noises and were scared to be there late at night. But just because a place can seem menacing with the lights off does not necessarily mean it is haunted. I was told by this individual that Theater Four, located in the back of the building, was the creepiest of them all, and where people felt some kind of energy.

After years of stories, including that of a murder on site, we investigated it in 2020. A couple of our Ghosts on the Coast crew were friends with the owner of the theater at the time. Since it was closed down post-Covid and about to be transitioned to a new operator, he gave us total access to the entire theater. He opened up for us, let us in, and then left us to have the place to ourselves for a few hours. This was after giving us some information. The building dates to 1912 and there was indeed a Prohibition-era murder to occur in the back of the property when it was once an auto mechanic shop. The exact spot? Where the screen for Theater Four is. The owner at the time? John Snedecker.

Most of our investigation would be concentrated in Theater Four, but the same spirits who gave workers such an ominous feeling over the years were not as active with our group. Joining us were Roy and Joanne Dellosso, along with Lou Fligor, all of whom I met and became friends with through my work with the AHHS. They were present for so many amazing moments to come in the final chapters of this book. Joanne brought along a half-empty bottle of whiskey, hoping it would serve as a trigger object for the Prohibition-era ghosts. We did not drink any.

We received a steady stream of responses through the SB-7 for the duration of our investigation, which lasted for several hours. However, we were not able to piece anything together like in the previous chapter where the answers made clear sense. There was a string of names to be spoken, including "Wilson," "Mike," "Richard," "Chuck," and "Joel," but no explanations offered as to who these individuals were. Former mobsters who used the building as their stomping grounds back in the day? Past theater workers who still want to hang around to watch films in the afterlife? Or just spirits passing through with no set destination? We were also hoping to find the name of the murder victim, but it was to no avail.

The only interesting moment was towards the end of the investigation when I directly asked, "Do you know who John Snedecker is?" and the volume on the Spirit Box dropped down to the point where it was almost inaudible. This was intriguing because once the volume is set on the device itself, there is no way to lower it except by physically pressing the buttons, not through the speaker, and it is not Bluetooth compatible. The batteries for both were also fully charged, and after a few moments, began working again like normal. This could have just been a technical malfunction, but the timing makes us have to consider the possibility that maybe Snedecker was trying to get through to us.

Overall, the process ended up being more fun than the end result. We could not say either way if the theater is haunted. Since most of the people I have spoken to regarding paranormal experiences there I have personally known for a long time, I do believe them. But on this particular day, we just were not receiving anything with clarity. It was fun getting to walk around this large, historic theater by ourselves and with the lights off most of the time. We got to go behind some of the screens and in the projection rooms— we really left no stone unturned. We had extra EMF detectors on hand that day, brought along by Roy and Joanne, but neither of them were triggered to the point of intrigue.

Most people do not know of the murder in Theater Four. When I was assisting with a film screening of *House on Haunted Hill* as a fundraiser for the AHHS two years later, I discussed the murder in front of a packed house. I pointed to someone random in the audience and said in a sinister tone, "And it happened right where you're seating, madam!" She laughed and squirmed. I then informed her that it was a joke, and actually happened behind where I was standing while introducing the movie. Guests were curious. It made the evening, along with the legendary Vincent Price. Horror movies? Haunted theater? Crime scene of a century-old murder? The location which is now SmodCastle Cinemas should check all the boxes for the darker personalities out there. People like me.

While some murders manage to slip through the cracks, there were several more high-profile killings in town during Prohibition. Along with Genovese and Richard, there was a mobster named Al Lillien who was rumored to have a larger operation than any of them in smuggling illegal alcohol into the United States through Atlantic

Highlands. He lived at the former Hammerstein Mansion, situated high up in the Beacon Hill area of Atlantic Highlands. The geographic location, combined with the size of the mansion, made it the perfect place to be if you needed to see the bay where your imports would be coming in.

In another scene straight out of Hollywood, Lillien transformed the former theatrical producer's mansion into a veritable compound and factory for booze. An elevator shaft was installed which could fit an entire car, so it could be lowered into the basement, loaded, and brought back to the surface again ready to deliver goods. There was also a subterranean complex of sorts, where liquor was produced and bottled. Lillien drove a car that was fitted to have turrets for two machine guns in the back and had constant protection from bodyguards.

But all his money, guns, and guards could not keep him safe forever. In March 1933, someone finally decided to do away with Lillien. Whether he had grown too powerful or angered some of the wrong people, he was gunned down at his home in a murder that is still unsolved today. The shooter fired three bullets into Lillien's neck from the back and left a pair of pallbearer's gloves and an ace of spades by the body. How the case managed to not be solved was partly due to the shadowy involvement and/or ignorance of law enforcement. Atlantic Highlands police, they were told, could not investigate the murder because, despite the address, it was really a Middletown property. Middletown police then did not investigate and turned to the county, who failed to conduct a thorough investigation. His mansion burned down years later, leaving no remnants to be examined today.

Lillien's murder had occurred right as Prohibition was winding down. In the decade prior, Atlantic Highlands had been comparable to the Wild West in terms of shootouts. To onlookers and townspeople, these bursts of violence would have appeared to be at random. In 1923, a particularly fearsome and brutal gangster named Frank LeConte arrived in the area from Newark. He personally targeted trucks carrying booze and not only took the cargo, but made sure to execute the drivers and keep the trucks for himself. LeConte was given a taste of his own medicine in a shootout at the Atlantic Highlands Train Station. This was located where the parking lot for the harbor is now.

LeConte was not a bootlegger or rumrunner but was known as "hijacket" (which we would call a "hijacker" today) because his business was specifically tailored for stealing the goods of others and not importing his own. The gun battle left him dead and caused the wounding of six others. There was death and destruction all over the Bayshore, but no worse than Atlantic Highlands. Sharpshooters discovered that they could perch themselves up on Ocean Boulevard and take shots at the ships of opposing gangs and patrolling Coast Guard vessels.

While we cannot investigate the sites of Lillien's or LeConte's murders, they are still important because they convey that when walking around today in modernity, we must try to remember all that happened before, and why some towns or geographic regions may be more haunted than others. Just as there are likely bodies of sailors from past centuries buried all up and down the coast, there are also crime scenes that have come and gone and been forgotten. People always expect a "haunted" house or building to have a certain look, but in the end, it is about that past imprint.

Monmouth County has done an overall excellent job promoting its history, but it is not without shortcomings. There are markers all over dealing with the American Revolution, with something so simple as a campsite for one of the armies having a sign for it. But there are no markers for Prohibition, and none for these sometimes-spectacular gun battles and murders, which do deserve to have their sites noted. Did this start out as intentional, with people desperately wanting to forget past crimes? Or was it an innocent slipping through the cracks as time marched on?

The locations in this chapter are far from frightening: a school, a church thrift shop, a restaurant, and a movie theater. However, it is not about their current use, but what went on previously. Part of the reason why people surmise that the dead stick around is because of unfinished business or something disconcerting happening to them in their lives that they just cannot get over. Atlantic Highlands being a war zone during Prohibition fosters that atmosphere. The ghosts can be lingering anywhere.

Mobster Andy Richard himself is standing to the right, pictured here with two unknown individuals. (*Patti Wallace*)

The interior of Richard's liquor store which eventually became a speakeasy and then Andy's Tavern. More recent iterations include the Memphis Pig Out and now Atlantic House. (*Patti Wallace*)

The dining room of the now-defunct Memphis Pig Out in 2015. Ellie Huson's yellow chair can be seen to the left. Note the ceiling was still intact from the days of Andy's Tavern. (*Memphis Pig Out Facebook*)

*Above:* A postcard of the Thrift Shop when it was owned by actor Robert Mantell and named "Brucewood." Richard later purchased the property and made several changes and additions. (*Atlantic Highlands Historical Society*)

*Right:* The basement of Richard's former mansion home, now the St. Agnes Thrift Shop. If there were any tunnels stemming from this area, they have long been cemented over.

**9**

# DON'T GO IN THE HOUSE

## DEMPSEY HOUSE, LEONARDO, AND AUTHOR'S HOME, HOLMDEL

Horror movies have ingrained into our minds what a haunted location should look like. As paranormal investigators, we also make judgments when approaching a house or building. Some have the look and some do not. The place I have investigated the most in my life is the Strauss Mansion Museum in Atlantic Highlands, which I am saving as the "best for last" at the end of this book. That place looks haunted. People enter it, mainly for non-paranormal events, with a look on their faces that they are about to experience something ghostly. A horror movie titled *Don't Go in the House* was filmed there in 1979 when it was still a private residence. It was the perfect set.

This was a feeling I assuredly did not have when I first entered my own home in 2018. My father had passed away the previous year. We were living in Hazlet and my mother and I decided to move following his death, which was not an easy decision, but one that had to be. We looked at a rental in the next town over in Holmdel, which was an unassuming townhouse with neighbors on both sides. Had I been in a better frame of mind, I might have looked at each house or apartment with an eye for, "Is this place haunted?" But I was not in that mindset. We moved in during the spring. Nothing was awry. It was as average as a house could be. But then by fall, something changed within it.

There should have been no reason for this. Being a rental, we did not make any changes to the house, nor did we do any painting. Homeowners routinely say that renovations, small or large, can bring out ghostly activity. None of this was happening here. But we started to hear noises. There was banging on the front door, which I ran to, making sure to see if it was a person outside. While sitting downstairs, I could hear the floor above me creaking. Our cat became fixated on the stairs, where he would sit at the top and stare down for hours on end, something he did not do at our previous house.

It got to the point where I did something that I always said I would never do at my own house, which was to investigate. I attempted a couple of Spirit Box sessions but there was nothing but straight radio static. It was now October, and in the midst of a full month of paranormal events, I thought why not finally try a wine glass séance.

My partner and I set one up in the kitchen. The glass started to move and something came through. It was, so it told us, the spirit of a man who died in the house. It would not tell us a name or anything specific other than he was sick before he passed away. There were then three or four quick knocks on the glass of the back door that caught us so off-guard that we both jumped. The curtains were closed but we went over as fast as possible and ripped them open to see if someone was playing a prank with us that happened to coincide with this séance. No one was there.

A day or two after, one of our neighbors was outside and I asked about some of the past tenants. Our house had always been used as a rental, and it was never lived in by the owners. Judging by how much mail we were receiving for others, there had been a fair amount between 1993 when it was built and 2018 when we moved in. I asked if anyone had died in the house, and the look on my neighbor's face said it all. He did not remember much else.

Asking another neighbor churned up more information. There was a man, maybe in his late twenties or early thirties, who lived there briefly with his fiancée and a dog. He was a severe diabetic who had an incident of some kind when he was alone in the house one afternoon and died. The fiancée returned home that night to find him dead. Not one person I talked to could remember his name, but they recalled hearing the sound of his dog barking constantly that day until the fiancée arrived. I was also told she went off the deep end following his death, getting into drugs, trashing the place, and slashing up some of the walls before moving out.

By December, I invited the entire group over for a paranormal investigation. The Spirit Box was again quiet, but the séance was active. Still without giving us a name, he told us that he missed his dog and was waiting for the pet to pass on so he could join him. That was all we had, until Patty took a picture aimed up the stairs with her FLIR camera which detects heat signatures and forms an image based on that. At the top of the stairs appeared to be an almost human-like shape, as if someone was standing with their hands at their sides. Future pictures did not replicate the result, so this was not something in the wall, such as an electrical panel, that might throw off a change in temperature. Why all of this activity on the stairs? Is it possible that as he was dying, he tried to make it downstairs for help and died there? No one knew anything about what part of the house he died in.

All was pretty much quiet, with occasional unexplainable noises, for about a year or so. Patty then managed to find the obituary of the man who died in our house by using a paid subscription for a website that searches deaths based on addresses. We finally had a name, but it was eerie to see the face of what was possibly still lurking in our home. The obituary also mentioned the dog. It has been a long time now since anything strange has happened in this house. Maybe he was right, in that he was waiting for his dog to pass on and it finally did.

You would never in a million years enter my house and think that any paranormal activity would be occurring there. The same can be said for a few private residences our group has investigated over the years. Despite maybe getting some great evidence, people watch the videos and see the pictures and think, "That's not scary." The setting really does make or break the mood. Then there is the opposite, with a place simply known as the Dempsey House.

Located on a corner in Leonardo and nearly surrounded by trees is a small, sinister-looking peanut stone house with a large, rusted gate in front. But what this building lacks in size, it exceeds in stories. Almost Whipporwill-esque in nature, people in the surrounding area have grown up with all kinds of lurid tales of murder and suicide. There is no set time period for when the multiple legends were to unfold, though the house dates back to 1926.

Late one night, "Old Man Dempsey" woke up from his sleep, lost his mind, and decided to murder his entire family. There are no specifics on how many people this would have been. He either used a shotgun or an ax to do the deed. He then became so overcome with grief after committing the murder that he killed himself, either by turning the gun around or by hanging. Most say he threw a rope up to one of the lower tree branches and hanged himself to death. Depending on who is telling the story, some may add the cheerful nugget that it was Halloween, and numerous trick-or-treaters passed by for hours into the night, seeing his dead body swinging and assuming it was just a realistic decoration.

The first time I heard about this place, I was told the initial police officer to arrive at the scene was so startled by what he saw, between the family being chopped to pieces and the culprit dead outside, that the cop became so traumatized that he too killed himself. There is a third version that states Mr. Dempsey was not a murderer, but his wife was. He had been ill for some time, unable to get out of bed and care for himself. One day, Mrs. Dempsey had enough, and never returned to his aid. He was left to starve to death in bed. The officer in this one was also driven into some kind of madness upon entering the house and after seeing his decomposing corpse, pulled his gun out, stuck it into his own mouth, and pulled the trigger.

You could probably walk the streets of Leonardo today and ask people, "Tell me about the Dempsey House," and get a slightly different story from every one of them. Each person adds their own flavor based on what they themselves were told. The versions documented by *Weird N.J.* over the years are just a small sampling. The school I worked at was only 2 miles away. Many of my students were from Leonardo, which is the next town over from Atlantic Highlands, and some of them also had different stories.

Where do we start when breaking this one down? Like Whipporwill, but unlike the Spy House, there is no singular direct source. There really was a Dempsey family, but they lived across the street in a normal house. What is referred to today as the "Dempsey House" was nothing more than a water pump house built over a well. This offered clean water to their family and other residents before a municipal system was constructed. It is known that no one ever lived at this house, and since any murder mentioned would have had to occur post-1926, they would not be merely just legends if they happened.

The origin of the property is well-documented and is so far from frightening that it is almost ironic. While today, people pass by the house and think back to the poor family that was murdered by their insane father, the specific area that the house was built had happiness for children in mind instead of their destruction. Before being sold to the Dempsey Family in 1920, the land was owned by Charles DuVale who was a broker on Wall Street. His considerable wealth led him to construct a private play area for the children of Leonardo, complete with a swimming pool, slide, bowling alley, "teeter board," merry-go-round, and playground.

A *Monmouth Press* article from 1914 mentions the construction of these items, and also notes the building of a "waterworks" and that "refreshing ice water" was on hand to keep the children hydrated in the sweltering summer heat. This could be a reference to the spring, upon which a well and, later, the pump house was built by the Dempseys after they purchased the property.

Unfortunately, William DuVale did meet a tragic end in 1918. He was found dead early one morning by his family in their house across from the recreation area. There had been a gas leak from the stove in the kitchen. According to reports, the fumes were so severe that as soon as he opened the door to go into the kitchen, they hit him like a wave, and he fell to the floor unconscious and asphyxiated soon after. He left behind an estate of $5,000,000. Four years earlier, the DuVales experienced another death in their house. While caring for their ill seven-year-old nephew, he succumbed to pneumonia on the premises. Neither of these deaths seem to be the starting point for the swirl of rumors.

Over the years, as water was available throughout the town, there was no need for the pump house, and it was left abandoned. With weeds overgrown, the trees seeming to overtake the building and swallow it whole, the massive gate growing rusty, and the house with boarded up windows gradually fading into disrepair, it began to perfectly look the part of a place that must be haunted. It was also a prime target for exploration by kids of the neighborhood.

While stories of witches and devil worship were perhaps told about Whipporwill to keep people away, so too were stories of murder, suicide, and madness passed down from one generation to another by residents of Leonardo who probably just wanted to keep their children from breaking into the house and getting in trouble. Such a situation is like so many others, in that it backfired. It did not keep people from wanting to accept the challenge of breaking into the ghostly old shack, it made them want to do it even more.

I have never been inside the house. Last I heard from someone who worked for Middletown Township (who has owned the property since 2004 when it was sold by Michael Dempsey whose father William acquired it from the DuVale estate), it was unsafe due to a rotting floor. This was years ago, and it is probably much worse now. As for what will become of the property, it is hard to say. In 2021, it was awarded a $15,000 historic preservation grant by the New Jersey Historic Trust. The house is now officially known in legal paperwork as the "Dempsey Pump House," and there were plans as of that moment to nominate the site to be on the National Register of Historic Places.

It does not seem that $15,000 will go a long way, though the building is not that big. I also do not know if there is enough history for it to be considered historic at the national level. But maybe through this process, the house can get restored and the property tidied, and turned into a park or community center which can be enjoyed by all. Such an idea would fit in line with William DuVale's original intent. The notoriety may be ruined by restoration, but I would love to go inside, as would countless others. After years of hearing the stories and wondering what the interior might look like, perhaps within a few more years it will become a reality.

My team and I have filmed videos there explaining the legends, but we have never conducted an actual investigation. Since not only did anyone not die there, but did not live either, I never had quite the push. There is no way to stand near the house without crossing over the wall that semi-surrounds the property. It is also quite open to the neighborhood, and the amount of time we would have to spend there may trigger someone into thinking we were trying to break in. Looking back on it now, I would like to reach out to the ghost of William DuVale and ask what he thinks of his idea for joy and happiness turning into a wonderland of deathly legends and folklore. Unfortunately for him, some places just look the part, and the Dempsey House will always be a source of intrigue throughout the year, especially on Halloween, for the people of Leonardo and all paranormal enthusiasts.

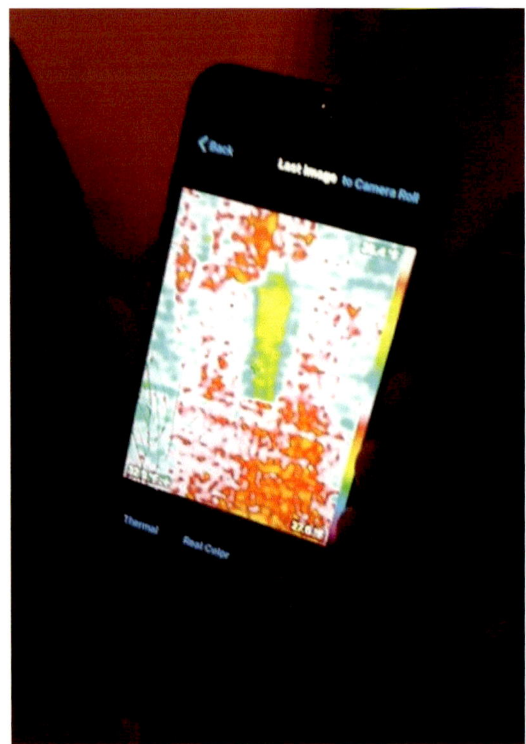


*Left:* During an investigation at my own house, we gathered around to view the figure-like image standing at the top of my stairs captured by Patty's FLIR camera.

*Below:* A view of the Dempsey House from the street, September 2023. It has the allure of a house that should be haunted.

*Above:* The front gate to the Dempsey House has gone missing (or was removed) in the last couple of years, as has the wrought-iron "D" that once adorned it. I took this picture standing where the gate used to be.

*Right:* While this was definitely a swimming pool, it is currently unknown if this was the one constructed by Charles DuVale or was added later on by the Dempseys when they built the pump house. The stonework is identical but peanut stone is prevalent in the area and easily blended.

A close-up of the pool, which has become an area for stagnant water and garbage to collect. The pipes in the side wall come from the direction of the house, making it likely it was originally filled with water directly from the spring.

The west side of the Dempsey House, taken from the woods near the street. Do you dare go any closer?

**10**

# THE MYSTERY OF
# GREEN LIGHT CEMETERY

## BAY VIEW CEMETERY, LEONARDO

The locals call it "Green Light Cemetery." Located in the Leonardo section of Middletown a little over a mile away from the Dempsey House, Bay View Cemetery would appear to be nothing more than ordinary. But for as long as people can remember, witnesses have reported strange phenomena, from the ghost of an old caretaker with a lantern to a mysterious green light that seems to emanate from nowhere. Theories range from practical to outright bizarre. What exactly is going on here? Is it just a case of mass hysteria, or is something paranormal happening?

Bay View Cemetery was officially incorporated in 1889, though the land was used as a burying ground for almost a century before that. It contains nearly 4,000 graves. The oldest known, of a woman named Charlotte Beete, is from 1804. The saddest is much more recent, as there is a stone cross that simply reads "Baby Adams" which dates to April 1968 and memorializes an infant who lived less than one month. While Rose Hill has its areas that give off a creepy aura, the same cannot be said about this particular cemetery. The older sections manage to blend in with the new. If you did not hear anything about this place previously, you probably would not be walking around looking for something spooky to happen.

The most important person of local notoriety buried here may be Thomas Henry Leonard, the visionary businessman who founded Atlantic Highlands and whom Leonardo is named after. Through a series of land deals, Leonard turned a frontier-like bayshore town into a sprawling Victorian resort that at one time had an enormous variety of hotels and boarding houses in operation, the best beaches on the Jersey Shore, and countless attractions. He recognized Atlantic Highlands' proximity to New York City, and helped establish a ferry system that would bring in tens of thousands of summer vacationers to the area daily for more than three decades.

He predicted or hoped that "Monmouth County will someday be Monmouth City." While that was never quite achieved, there are few people who would have been able to pull off such a transformation. When he arrived in the area, the population was so sparse that his daughter noted in her own book that one night when their neighbor's house burned down, each home was so isolated from the others that no one heard a commotion or saw the glow from the blaze. Within a matter of years, there would be so many homes built that it would be hard to find a piece of ground without one.

Leonard was also a historian who chronicled the history of Monmouth County. His seminal work, *From Indian Trail to Electric Rail*, was published in 1923 and contained an early history of the region as well as updates that he personally witnessed during his life. For anyone researching what life was like in the past of Atlantic Highlands or the Bayshore, this document is essential reading.

Most famously, Bay View Cemetery contains the remains of world-famous Shakespearean theater actor Robert Bruce Mantell of Scotland who called the St. Agnes Thrift Shop his summer home for two decades. His acting troupe of more than thirty members toured the United States for years during the late Victorian era and into the twentieth century. They often stayed with Mantell on the third floor of his house during the summer season. Mantell made a career of churning out one legendary performance after another in such roles as *Othello*, *Hamlet*, *King Lear*, *Richard III*, and *Macbeth*, among many others both Shakespearean and non.

It has been suggested that Mantell's acting was so effective, if he had been younger and was able to devote more time to making silent films, his fame could have eclipsed that of Rudolph Valentino. He had a rich, booming voice that carried throughout the entire theater at a time before microphones. This talent, though, did not necessarily transfer to the silver screen where overly exaggerated facial expressions and gesturing were now seen up close and personal by the camera. This happened to many actors who tried to switch from stage to film. While he did not receive terrible reviews, they were not stellar either. He ended up making seven movies altogether, from 1915 until 1923, before dying at Brucewood in 1928. Along with Edwin Booth, Mantell is considered one of the finest theater actors of his generation and the last of the great tragedians. Having been born at the wrong time was what would lead to his now near obscurity.

Mantell's married life may be the most interesting part about him. He divorced his first wife, Marie Sheldon, in 1893 but failed to make alimony payments and was banned from acting in New York until he reached a large settlement with her in 1904. He then married actress Charlotte Behrens, whom he was having an affair with while married to Sheldon. She was married to another man at the time. Behrens had been his leading lady who was twelve years his junior. She died under mysterious circumstances in 1898 of a strange liver condition which gradually got worse and worse. Mantell had been on the road during most of her illness, visiting only on weekends, and was not with her when she died.

He married his next leading lady, who was twenty-one years younger, the following year. She had stepped in while Behrens was sick. This would be Marie Booth Russell who was mentioned in the last chapter and died on Halloween in 1911. Her illness was also believed to be strange, though today it is thought she had Bright's disease, which is a form of kidney failure sometimes caused by toxins. He was on the road when she died as well. Russell is interred at Bay View. Robert had erected a massive monument to her that reads, "In Memory of My Beloved Wife," along with her full name and the date of her death. However, his name is also inscribed on the stone underneath the quote as if to give him credit as the person dedicating it. His name is carved much larger than hers.

Further research revealed that he had an identical stone and inscription for Behrens made at her place of rest in Pennsylvania thirteen years earlier.

The trend continued a few months later, when Robert married Genevieve Hamper in 1912 who again was his leading lady who filled in while the other was sick. She was ahead of her time in regards to her treatment of stage acting and was thirty-four years younger than him. Genevieve had her own Shakespearean company and tried to change the acting methods of those in her troupe, as people were becoming accustomed to motion pictures and it was influencing the way they viewed drama. She and Robert were quite the virtuoso pair and used the barn on their property for this theatrical planning and rehearsing.

They had one son, Robert Jr., who ventured into acting but commit suicide in 1933 in Hollywood at age twenty-one after allegedly being unhappy with his career and failing to live up to expectations compared to his parents' success. He is buried with his father, while his mother lived until 1971 and is interred in New York. In a touch of irony, when Robert died, Genevieve married her leading man whom she was acting with while Mantell was not in good health and nearing the end of his life. This was long-time troupe member John Alexander.

This is all not to allege that Robert Mantell was a murderer or had anything to do with the death of two wives, but they both managed to die of organ failure while he was away on tour in much the same circumstances both in their lives and careers. It seemed to be a chain that repeated itself over and over again. He must have really loved Genevieve.

But the names of those resting at Bay View have taken a backseat to the countless stories of strange activity reported over the years, and the witnessing of a green light. Some have seen it beam through the trees that surround the cemetery, while others say it hovers over the land like a ghostly fog and casts a greenish glow on the many gravestones. Team member and long-time Atlantic Highlands Historical Society board of directors member Joanne Dellosso had her own experience with this green glow, saying she saw it with her friends in the 1970s. Rather than a steady beam, it was like a mist. It hovered and then dissipated. She also added that since the 1960s, it was "a popular place to bring your date for a good scare."

There are also tales of the ghost of an old caretaker, still performing his duties. He walks the cemetery at night, checking on the graves, while holding a green-lit lantern. Other legends state that his apparition is using the green light to guide the souls of the recently departed safely away to the afterlife. Regardless of what you have heard or believe, it is true that people have indeed seen something at Bay View Cemetery, or at least thought they did. Unlike other local legends and creepy points of interest, witness stories are not cryptic, anonymous, or far-fetched but very real. Many locals openly talk about the strange occurrences they have witnessed.

Can a practical explanation be found for what people have been seeing? One theory claims that as some of the older coffins and caskets begin to disintegrate, gasses and embalming fluid from the bodies seep into the ground and work their way up to the surface. In the right light or humidity of the air, this release might give the appearance of a floating green mist. I asked a local funeral director about this, and he said that nothing he could think of within embalming fluid itself could cause such a glow in any condition, and that if it could, such a phenomenon would be much more prevalent in cemeteries of similar age all over the country, not just at Bay View.

The most logical theory would seem to be the close proximity of an old lighthouse, named the Chapel Hill Rear Range Lighthouse, which is located above the cemetery on a hill. It operated from 1856 until 1957 and was a part of a lesser-known system of smaller lights on the Jersey Bayshore and Staten Island. The Conover Beacon of Leonardo a mile away would align with the Chapel Hill light indicating to ships where they were and whether they were safely sailing through the channel. The Chapel Hill Light still stands today deactivated and almost unidentifiable as a private residence, while the Conover Beacon remains in its original form and is currently under restoration after being abandoned for decades. Research does not indicate whether the Chapel Hill Light was tinted green but maybe an illusion or the beam passing through the foliage made it appear that way.

It would seem like the factoring of the Chapel Hill Light into this story would be the final word. However, it still fails to explain two things: 1) if the light was a steady beacon for over 100 years, how come its effect on the cemetery was not seen on a nightly basis and by more people, to the point where it would have been common knowledge and no legend would have ever developed? And 2) the light was deactivated in 1957, so what would account for all of the sightings since, as most experiences seem to be from the 1960s and beyond?

We may never know the real cause of this phenomenon, though we can safely say it is not leaking embalming fluid. There is nothing physically present at the cemetery itself that could cause a green light, unless you want to go a step further and say that the lighthouse above it is what is haunted and the light is still coming from there. As for a ghostly caretaker, maybe there was a cemetery worker who enjoyed his job so much in life that he wanted to keep watch over the cemetery in death. However, it would make more sense that someone was poking around there at night decades ago and was happened upon by an actual living caretaker (who would have had a lantern or flashlight) and returned to his or her friends to say they were scared by a ghost. It might have spiraled from there.

Joanne and I did a short investigation in 2019, and I returned with Patrick in 2023 for some location filming as we were preparing for a documentary. Neither time did anything creepy or paranormal happen, though there were a few isolated words in the Spirit Box session I conducted with Joanne. One presence intelligently repeated the word "Strauss" after she and I were talking about the museum, where we were going to be doing an investigation later that night with the rest of the group.

In all my research, I have not come across any witness statements of a green light newer than the 1980s. The location is not as popular as Whipporwill or the Dempsey House, both of which are only minutes away, but it does manage to still pop up online and in newspaper articles around Halloween as people reminisce about what they saw, or what their friends told them. If we think back to a setting being everything, Bay View is simply just not scary. That could be why interest has waned slightly, and there are not enough people actively seeking the mysterious green lights. It is also still active with modern burials and visits from grieving family members. For that reason, please be respectful if you go exploring.

*Right:* Thomas Henry Leonard, the visionary founder of Atlantic Highlands. (*From Indian Trail to Electric Rail*)

*Below:* A postcard featuring Robert Mantell and two of his more famous roles, Richard III and Cardinal Richelieu. It is signed by the actor and inscribed, "There is no such word as fail." (*Emory University*)

Robert Mantell was the great-uncle of actress Angela Lansbury. Can you spot any resemblance? This portrait was taken in 1910. (*University of Washington*)

Marie Booth Russell in 1909. She is seen here so full of life, but would be dead within two years. (*New York Star*)

*Right:* The grave of Marie Booth Russell at Bay View Cemetery, dedicated to her by her husband, Robert Mantell.

*Below:* Mantell and his fourth (and final) wife, Genevieve Hamper, pose for this romantic image by the fireplace at their Atlantic Highlands home in 1918. (*Robert Mantell's Romance*).

The same fireplace today, at the St. Agnes Thrift Shop. Robert Mantell's memory is honored with a photo of him on the center of the mantle.

*Above:* The Chapel Hill Rear Range Lighthouse when it was still in operation. This building would have loomed over the cemetery. Could its beacon, when in operation, be the cause of the mysterious green light? (*United States Coast Guard*)

*Right:* The nearby Conover Beacon in Leonardo, which would have worked in conjunction with the Chapel Hill Light to guide ships in the Bayshore.

## 11

# THE MOST HAUNTED HOUSE IN NEW JERSEY?

## PART 1

## STRAUSS MANSION MUSEUM, ATLANTIC HIGHLANDS

By the fall of 2022, the Strauss Mansion had been labeled the "Most Haunted House in New Jersey" by several prominent local newspapers and magazines. It also managed to be featured in a segment on *News 12 New Jersey*. The masses were finally learning what my crew and I had already known for a decade, and others for far longer than that. It is difficult to concretely say that the Strauss Mansion, or any house for that matter, is "most haunted," but as you will see in the next two chapters, the longest and most in-depth in this book, something special is definitely happening here.

The following pages will read like a compendium, but keep in mind the reason I have so many stories to document is just because of the sheer amount of time I have spent at this location, both working, running paranormal events, and conducting our own research. This may give readers the false notion that this house is literally spouting paranormal activity when that is not the case. Like all haunted buildings, the number of quiet nights and investigations where nothing happens far outweigh the good times.

My association with the Atlantic Highlands Historical Society began by accident. I was still heavily involved with the Proprietary House when I visited the Strauss Mansion in July of 2013 with Jake and Jeff for one of their Sunday afternoon open houses. I had only learned about the existence of this place from parents at the school, one of which asked if I would consider volunteering there for Halloween tours. I already had too much going on, so that was not possible, but I did want to visit and check the place out, and also see if it was haunted. When the three of us arrived, we realized that the tours were self-guided and we were given a pamphlet and allowed to walk around the massive 21 room Victorian mansion on our own. Such a notion was perfect, and these style tours still continue today. They give visitors a chance to take their time and explore, as opposed to being rushed from room to room.

Jake and I left our phone recorders running in an attempt to capture EVPs, which was to no avail. However, I had recently downloaded a new app called "Ghost Radar" to my phone and was walking around with it scanning. I have never fully believed this

154

app to be real, more like a game or gimmick, but there have been times that the words which appear on screen match up to what is going on in real life. For example, on this first visit, as I walked into the Tower Room on the third floor, the word "tower" came up on the screen.

When we were finished, I asked the person docenting if the place was haunted. He informed us that while he never personally experienced anything, several board members had, and the museum occasionally allowed paranormal groups to come in and investigate. We exchanged contact information, and soon arranged for our group to come in and investigate the next month. Little did I know that I was about to be just as involved here as I was at the Proprietary House in only a matter of a few months.

I had always been interested in the Revolutionary War, so getting accustomed to this new history took time. The Proprietary House was focused on one person, while the Strauss Mansion was more about an era and way of life, and also telling the story of an entire town through various exhibits and collections set up in the many rooms. Navigating the house early on was like a maze. Every room was connected to each other, which I had found out was so the servants could move around doing their duties without bumping into their employer in the main hallway. It also helped with ventilation and cooling the house down in the summer. The tower originally had a removable cap, which, when lifted, allowed more cooling air to enter through the top of the house and circulate downward like a nineteenth-century form of air-conditioning. There was a separate servants' staircase that led from the kitchen to the second floor. But why such a large house and need for servants?

The namesake of what would become a museum in the 1980s was Adolph Strauss, a German-Jewish immigrant who founded an extremely successful business on 49th Street in New York. It was there he sold "notions," such as small nick-nacks and harmonicas. While we refer to the building today as a "mansion," the Strausses intended it to be merely their "summer cottage" where they would spend weekends to escape the blistering heat in the city. Their wealth was evident, to have such a house constructed only to inhabit it approximately twenty days a year. Strauss contracted architect Solomon Cohen and builder Adolph Huntera at the end of 1892 to have the house finished by June 1893, in which they would receive a bonus for completing it in only six months or pay a penalty if they did not. This was a feat they accomplished.

The team of Cohen and Huntera built another similar mansion which is visible from the second and third floors of the Strauss Mansion. While the hillside of Atlantic Highlands today is considered historic and the most desirable area to live in town, in the 1890s, that was not the case. While operating as a thriving resort town with hotels, restaurants, and all kinds of attractions hosting thousands of people a day, non-whites and non-Protestants were not welcome to stay at hotels or live near the center of town, and therefore had to stay on the outskirts. The hillside was considered far enough away. Most, if not all, neighbors of the Strausses early on were Jewish, including some of their own friends who worked in close proximity to his company on 49th Street in Manhattan.

Along with his wife, Jeanette Rosenthal, and likely visits from his children (who were all adults by the time the cottage was constructed), Adolph lived opulently and entertained guests throughout the summer. Unfortunately, personal records have been lost to time, but it can be speculated that many of their high society friends would have joined them. Along with being a businessman, he was a philanthropist who raised money for numerous charities, a hospital, and was active in helping to garner donations for the building of the tomb of Ulysses S. Grant which was finished in 1897.

There are remnants of call bells for servants located around the house, as well as pipes for gas lights which have been capped. As the residence was constructed with only summers in mind, there are just two fireplaces, located downstairs. These would have been a little more than decorative, also lit by gas. A stained-glass window over the original front door is inscribed "A.S" and there are several additional beautifully crafted stained-glass windows throughout the first floor, and one in the second-floor bedroom. Though not used as the entrance today, the wood-paneled foyer would have been seen as grand and luxurious.

But this magnificent mansion was not enjoyed for long by the Strausses. Jeanette died in 1900, and then Adolph in 1905. His family sold the property to Ferdinand Minroth in 1907, who physically left his mark by carving an "F.M." into one of the cedar shake shingles on the side of the house. All told, there would be ten different owners, with the AHHS being the longest-tenured and final. For private residents, Axel and Gertrude Komstedt lived there the longest, twenty-one years dating from 1923–1944.

Perhaps the most influential of all owners was the family who ended up selling the property to the historical society, which had the goal of restoration and turning it into a museum headquarters in mind. The use of the word influential to describe them is not a positive one. From June 1, 1970 until December 30, 1980, the Strauss Mansion was owned by Fun Wah and Mary Ann Chin. He owned a Chinese restaurant and also taught private cooking classes locally. It was he and his wife who allowed the house to fall into such disrepair that the town of Atlantic Highlands had condemned it and wanted it demolished for safety reasons.

The Chins had also operated it as unsanctioned apartments, which will be the source of one or more ghostly entities in the pages to come. It is possible that the building was used as apartments before they purchased it, and they kept this going. To say apartment was putting it nicely, as it was more of a flophouse with drug addicts and people down on their luck looking for a place to stay temporarily. This is not hearsay, but what neighbors remember.

The once-magnificent rooms became dilapidated, and the former third-floor servants' quarters, which contained the largest of such apartments, was littered with graffiti and engravings on the walls. These can still be seen today, as funding has not been available to fix that last portion of the house. While unsightly, they have proved valuable when trying to address the ghosts because of the numerous names the writing contains.

In 1979, shortly before the house was sold, a B-level exploitation horror movie, *Don't Go in the House*, was filmed there. This is a film which later achieved cult status and was placed on England's infamous "Video Nasty" list. Several townspeople acted as extras, and a few people I know personally remember when the movie was being shot. Some vaguely remember the Chins, though no one can pinpoint exactly how that house came to be used for the film. Judging by the many uses of fire throughout, it might be a comically reasonable assumption to think that the owners were hoping the house would burn down to collect the insurance money.

There were no doubt many style changes made to the inside Strauss Mansion over the years, both good and bad. However, we do not have any existing photographs of the interior of the house from any of the previous ownerships. In fact, the only documented images of how it looked inside prior to 1980 come from the movie itself, which did no set decorating since the atmosphere was creepy enough and the house was supposed to be bordering on neglect. There are also only a few exterior photographs in existence as well, and we can see that not much has changed in the last 130 years.

The Strauss Mansion had several ghost stories associated with it prior to my arrival and involvement. As we first investigated in August of 2013, I heard some of these from Roy, Joanne, and another board member Lou Fligor. They had run Halloween-themed lantern tours every year for decades, where guides would lead groups around the house and actors would jump out and scare them. It was usually after such events that strange activity would occur. In the Tower Room, there is an old basketball trophy from the local high school which is nailed to the wall. One night, while on the floor below, Roy heard a bang and scraping noise. He went upstairs a few minutes later to not only find the trophy had fallen off the wall, but was out in the hallway, at least 10 feet away.

In that same room a few years later, they had strapped a creepy looking animatronic figure (named "Donna the Dead") up in the tower with a spotlight aimed at it so people could see it from far away. This figure was knocked loose, falling into the light which subsequently burned a hole in the floor. It was only by coincidence that a volunteer was going up there to see why the spotlight had shut off, did they see smoke and start alerting others to help put out the fire. Prior to this, another paranormal group had investigated the Strauss Mansion and captured an EVP of a little girl speaking about a fire. Was this a warning or premonition?

Unlike so many haunted historic sites, it was interesting to listen to experiences from the people who actually had them, not something that had been passed down over forty years with no way to trace the source. Joanne's dog used to come inside while she was docenting and frequently sat next to the Chickering grand piano in the parlor with its head cocked as if listening to music. Over the years, many people have heard the faint sounds of that piano playing, though it is extremely old and only has two working keys. An EVP that Patty captured in 2017 sounded like someone slamming down on the keyboard, though the noise produced certainly seems like more than those two keys. Our group was seated in the room when it happened and did not hear anything with the naked ear.

We arrived for our first investigation in 2013 with some of these in mind. Joining me was Brett, Jake, and our friends from the Proprietary House board, Carla and Doug Balduini, who stepped in for Jeff who could not make it. The night had a bunch of little moments, but nothing overwhelming. There were some footsteps and scuffling, which could have been squirrels running up the side of the house as they are known to do but it did sound like it was coming from inside. Before Carla and Doug arrived, there was knocking at the back door, to which I started walking to thinking it was them trying to get in, but no one was there. It is hard to call bumps, knocks, and noises serious paranormal evidence. We left there that night not quite sure what to make of the Strauss Mansion. Was it even haunted? The ghosts, if there were any, had themselves a quiet night.

Two months later, midway through October, I resigned from the Proprietary House because it was getting to be too much. The same night I came to that decision, I gave a call to the parent who had wanted me to volunteer. I figured that I would have the time now and this would not entail much. She was ecstatic and told me they were meeting the next day to go over the haunted house tour script and do readings. Just like that, in a matter of twenty-four hours, I went from one museum to the next, but I was not anticipating what was to come.

I helped with the Halloween tours and had a blast. I also came to know Roy, Joanne, and Lou as good friends. They asked if I would be interested in volunteering and I said yes, though I was not looking for a major commitment. I attended their next board meeting with my résumé. I remember leaving my house that night and my father remarking, "Why are you bringing a résumé if you are not going to join?" I affirmed that I was just bringing it so they could learn about me and that I was not joining another board, just looking to help. "You'll join," he said. Dad was indeed right.

Just like the Proprietary House, I was asked to overhaul social media for the organization as well as their communications through email blasts. They also asked if I had any fundraising ideas since they were preparing for the next museum season. The first that came to mind was doing public paranormal investigations where we would charge people a donation, give them a tour and a talk about ghost hunting, and let them investigate. These would not be like the scripted Halloween tours, but actual paranormal investigations where people would hopefully experience something. I also wanted to try them in the spring and summer when there was not much competition. This was approved, with two scheduled for May 2014. They sold out quickly, and we added two more for June.

To make these more interesting from a storytelling and evidence perspective, I needed to have experiences of my own to talk about. I was told that my team and I (which would grow to encompass several board members) could investigate the Strauss Mansion whenever we wanted. I got right to it, at the end of 2013, which coincided with us getting our first SB-7 Spirit Box as well as other pieces of technology such as K2 and EMF readers, and a friend lending us a night-vision monocular.

Shortly after acquiring the SB-7, we recorded a response that is still one of our most profound ever captured. As Jake and I were in the basement doing a session, we were overcome with a feeling of dread at the same time. This is something that can occasionally happen due to paranormal energy, and there is nothing psychic about it. This led me to ask, "Are you mad at us?" to which a little girl responded with a slow and faint "Yeah." A man's voice is then heard saying "choke," and not hearing this at the time, I ask, "What do you want to do?" and the same male says a fragmented "to kill." This was one of those recordings that did not need much analysis, because it was clear as day. I do not think they were talking to us. Perhaps we stumbled into a conversation or argument on the other side.

A couple of months later, I headed up to the mansion during the afternoon. I had just finished teaching a class and had to be back at the school again in a few hours for a hockey game. I figured I would take a walk around and look in the library or office for something to do to kill time. As it happens, I ended up sitting on one of the couches in the parlor and fell asleep. I awoke maybe twenty minutes later to the boisterous sound of women laughing and talking, like it was coming from upstairs. My first thought was that other volunteers or board members had come in to work, and I shot right up and went upstairs. But as I made it to the staircase, I realized there was nothing in the house but dead silence. I went up anyway, and discovered that I still was the only person there.

Aside from the few examples of disembodied voices or noises at the Proprietary House, this was the only other time I heard something that clear.

By May 2014, the sold out public paranormal investigations began. We did provide the disclaimer that there was no guarantee of activity but we were hopeful. The participants were pleased with what happened, with everyone seated quietly together on the first floor and hearing what sounded like talking coming from upstairs. We also had a laser grid aimed at the stairs which can detect shadow movements if anything walks by, and something did break the grid momentarily in full view of everyone.

The night ended with several EMF detectors capturing steady readings and one participant being seemingly followed around the house. Every time someone took a picture of him, there were orbs in the frame. In one instance, his name came through on the SB-7 and I just happened to take a photo in his direction at the same time. Three orbs surrounded him.

The wine glass séances we conducted in ensuing months were also fruitful. Our group, in our own investigations, had begun talking to a ghost named "Bob" starting a few weeks prior. He was active, coming through and talking to the people, but other spirits were as well. A family who came to one of the public investigations later rented the Strauss Mansion so they could do their own. It was at this that they felt they were possibly talking to a dead relative. It was a young son who had died fifteen years earlier in a tragic accident and had never been to the Strauss Mansion before. The answers given during the séance, which included myself and my team members taking part, were unknown to everyone except the actual family of the deceased. The glass was sliding around the table at speeds we had yet to see, and it was both exciting and sad to watch, as were the family's incredulous reactions.

The most important moment during this investigation, though, would end up being something that I talk about at every paranormal lecture I have ever given and featured in my first book as an example of what can happen when you let the excitement of an investigation take hold of your analytical senses. It happened in the parlor. I was standing by a couch near the table we had set up for the séances and to hold our equipment. Lou was sitting, facing me, near the fireplace. Looking at him, to my right, was Jake, sitting on another couch. Lou then snapped a picture and exclaimed that an apparition was present. It was almost too good to be true.

Floating above Jake was a mist, and emerging from that was a clearly defined head and face. It was male. The eyes were closed, and the expression was tranquil. This all happened right after we finished a séance when we were possibly speaking to this family's deceased son. It stunned everyone in the room, including myself. The skeptic in me had to find an earthly explanation. Surely Jake had been standing up and happened to sit down at the exact moment Lou took the picture. That would account for the visual. But there was one problem with that, because Jake was seated the entire time. We scanned through pictures taken by Lou seconds earlier, who took several in quick succession. It could not have been Jake, and it was not a prank because I was staring right at the camera when he took the shot. This image temporarily became our "Holy Grail" because it was the best thing we had ever seen.

We posted it to Facebook and people were astounded. Likes and shares poured in. No one questioned the validity of the image, until Carly Vena reached out to me a few days later. The professional photographer, friend, camera expert, and self-proclaimed photography nerd was so captivated by what she saw that she wanted to take a look at the specs of the original image file. This would be so we could have an explanation and proof to combat any naysayers or those accusing us of fakery. As it turns out, in this gracious moment of reaching out to help us, she ended up debunking the image. There was no ghost present after all, and it was Jake himself. But if he was sitting still the whole time, how could this be so?

She determined that Lou's shutter speed on his camera had been set to 2.5 seconds, and the mere act of him pushing the button to take the picture nudged it just enough that it put Jake in two places at the same time. She provided a lengthy analysis, including highlighting areas of the image where other people too had moved, though they did not end up looking as ethereal as him. The way the light was aimed at Jake, combined with how he was positioned (plus wearing a light gray sweatshirt), gave him a ghostly aura and not one person online, including known skeptics who I know saw the image, had anything negative to say about the original picture. Thus, it became a learning experience to not get ahead of ourselves and to always do the extra work and analysis before publishing something as paranormal. I use this story today for that very reason. It is better to capture nothing at all than to share suspected evidence that has not been properly vetted.

Though not paranormal, the time at around when this image was taken marked a change at the Strauss Mansion, as our experiences were going to soon become better and more frequent. Our conversations with this entity named Bob were occurring both through the Spirit Box and also our séances. Through these numerous moments, we were able to ascertain (by him telling us) that he died in the house in the 1970s of a drug overdose in the third-floor bathroom. He was also a fan of rock music and Bob Dylan was his favorite singer. Bob became someone who we frequently greeted upon entering the house and we looked forward to chatting with him. We believed he was one of many tenants who used the Strauss Mansion under Chin's ownership and came to the conclusion that most of the ghosts were from this era.

In July 2014, I began to write my first book. I had enough experiences, combined with some sections on how to investigate plus my own personal philosophy, to complete the project. At this point, not many people knew about Bob, only my team and a few board members. During a film festival at the harbor on a warm evening that month, the AHHS had set up a table to hand out pamphlets about the organization. I was working a few tables down, helping a friend out with her restaurant's booth. A couple of hours later, the person who was president of the society at the time approached me with a confused and subdued look on her face.

She pointed a man out in the crowd, who I could barely make out because there were so many people. She asked if I knew him, and I said I did not. She laughed and then asked again, being certain that this gentleman must have been a friend of mine. Again, I reiterated that I had never seen him before in my life. She added that she thought he was my friend and that I "sent him over to play a joke" on her, and then, "He knows about Bob." My initial reaction was not very severe, even though not many people knew of his existence. I asked her what happened, and she told me how a conversation she had with this man, who had now disappeared into the crowd, transpired.

He approached her, asking if she was in charge of the historical society. When she said that she was, he then offered, "I will give you a thousand dollars if you stop allowing the paranormal investigations at the Strauss Mansion." Thinking it was a joke, she replied with a laugh, "How about five thousand?" The man was serious and said again that the investigations needed to stop. When she asked him why, he responded that many years ago he knew a man who lived on the third floor of the mansion and died of a drug overdose there. His name was Bob. This guy was also really nasty, according to him, and would probably do all kinds of terrible things to us during these investigations and he was concerned.

I found the entire situation amusing, but also odd. We had been speaking to Bob, but were skeptical of what he was telling us since sometimes ghosts will say anything or call themselves random names. Even with that bit of doubt, he was far from mean and angry. This information we learned did semi-prove that someone died of an overdose at this location, but why was it such a big deal to this individual? At another public paranormal investigation a few months later, we had an Atlantic Highlands police officer in attendance who was intrigued by the story.

He said he would look into it for us, checking death records, but if the apartments were unsanctioned and this person had no traceable family or identification, it is possible for him to have died with no record, newspaper article, or fanfare. The officer also told us that the first thing that came to mind when he heard this person trying to stop the investigations was that perhaps they had something to do with Bob's death and they were afraid Bob would communicate that to us during investigations.

This was something I never thought of, and so in our next investigation, we asked Bob who this man was, and Bob informed us that it was he who sold him the drugs that led to his overdose. Both myself and other members of Ghosts on the Coast have talked to an endless number of people over the years who lived in town during the 1970s and asked if they remembered anything like this happening. Only one person had a recollection from when they were a teenager. They lived up on the hillside and happened to see an ambulance in front of the mansion wheeling out a dead body under a blanket. Who this person was, there was no way to tell. Actual death records pertaining to the Strauss Mansion only show one documented death occurring there, of an elderly woman in the 1940s. But for reasons explained by the police officer, this record is no doubt incomplete.

The person to ask about this would have been Fun Wah Chin. For years, we attempted to find him through internet searches, if he was still alive at all. Nothing ever came up about him, and we had assumed he passed away. In 2021, during a film screening in October, Patty and I were sitting outside on the porch of the Strauss Mansion and she just happened to look him up again. Finally, there was some information, but it was unfortunately his obituary—from 2019. I sat straight up in my chair upon hearing this, because I was so disappointed that he had been alive all these years (living out of state) and we just did not know where to look to attempt to reach out to him. While it was nice to see a photograph of a past owner, it was such a letdown knowing that the one person who may have held the key to the identity of Bob and other spirits from that time period (distressed souls on drugs was a pretty good recipe for a haunting) was no longer around. Maybe he had information. Maybe some personal pictures of the mansion while he lived there. Maybe he could not have helped us at all, but it was a moot point now.

As my book was being finalized for publication in August 2014, a volunteer and I were attempting to clean the third-floor apartment area which had been used as storage for some time. There were boxes stacked from floor to ceiling, and when we pulled them away, it revealed more graffiti. This was not the first time it had been discovered, just the first time in a while that anyone had seen what was written. This was quite an eventful cleanup, as what we were about to see directly tied someone named Bob to this location. Among several names was, in fact, the name "Bob" written in chalk, along with the famous phrase from Bob Dylan's song "Rainy Day Woman #12 and 35," which was "Everybody Must Get Stoned." Maybe the ghosts were right after all.

Other names included Sherry, Lesley, Rob, Scott, and Chris either drawn in the same chalk, painted, or literally carved into the wall. Whether Bob knew these people, if they were all friends or roommates living together, and/or if they are alive today (a possibility) remains a mystery. However, I would think that after being open publicly for forty years, someone might have come around to the museum at some point and told whoever was docenting that they used to live at this location. Such an interaction has never occurred to my knowledge. They could also be spontaneous graffiti written by individuals breaking in during the period between when the Chins sold and transitioned the property to the AHHS in 1980, and the house was vacant for several months. There will never be a way to tell—that is, unless these people are still alive and reading this book and wish to contact me.

We headed into October 2014 with a full slate of events, which included the usual Halloween-themed tours as well as public investigations. The tours required an enormous amount of work, not just for acting but also the many volunteers who built sets and designed costumes. We spent many late nights there, and after most people had gone, we continued with our own investigations.

One night we ordered a pizza and were sitting in the parlor waiting for it to arrive. There were four or five of us, and someone had yelled out to the spirits to give a sign if they were there. On command, there was a light knocking noise. I was impressed because such moments are usually not so instantaneous. I then asked if they could do it again. They did. A few minutes later, there was a much louder knocking noise that came from what is now the front door. I got up, thinking it was the pizza being delivered, but no one was there. I sat back down, and the lights flickered.

There was something changing at the Strauss Mansion. Noises were becoming more frequent and the ghosts more informative. It was as if we could just snap our fingers and something was going to happen. All throughout this period of heightened activity, I kept thinking and asking myself if it was all really possible. Sure, the Proprietary House had its moments, but this was almost becoming too much. But I reminded myself that I was just spending so much time there, so it was easier to pick up on such incidents.

I was asked by the board to give a lecture on my book, which had been published the previous month, and also our ongoing investigations. This talk occurred on October 15, 2014. The crowd was enormous, and we ran out of chairs. I spoke for about an hour and then when my PowerPoint was done, I turned the lights back on and asked if anybody had any questions. After a few, one person in attendance asked me something which caught me off guard, because it came out of nowhere. "What do you think about demons?" was the question. I had not mentioned demons during my talk, nor do I ever usually because it is not something our group ever deals with. I did not really know what to say, and the first thought that came to mind was, "Well, first of all, there are no demons here." Before I could proceed with my explanation, something incredible happened.

At that very moment, a picture frame about 7 feet away from me slammed to the ground and ended up by my feet. It startled everyone and caused them to look where the sound came from. It is almost comical to think about now, how in unison, the heads of about fifty people turned to look at the wall, then all turned to look back at me, as if waiting for an explanation. The timing of the picture dropping was so precise that had we planned it as a gag, it would not have been nearly as perfect. I threw my arms in the air and shrugged my shoulders. People probably thought we had something to do with it, but we did not. I also never did finish answering the question, and the event came to an end. A volunteer, Chris Dubarton, who was sitting in a chair by this frame, shook his head and said, "Just a bad hook."

The frame was a small one, with the word "Parlor" enlarged in the middle, with a brief description for visitors so they would know what the room is and what it was used for. This did not just gently fall off the wall as if the nail it was on became weak. It impacted with such force that it appeared to have been yanked, and it landed by me. Upon examining the hole in the wall where it came from, there was a dent or cut angled downward, as if it was pulled. Normally, one could say that just the weight caused it to fall; however, there is hardly any weight to the picture at all.

A week later, following a night of tours and performances, some of the actors wanted to take part in a ghost hunt. Jake was in the parlor with them doing a séance and running the Spirit Box. Hunter and I were in the bathroom removing the makeup we had been wearing for our roles. As we scrubbed our faces, there was a creaking that came from inside the bathroom wall. I joked around that it was like the *House of Usher*, with the house groaning and starting to crumble, because it was a pronounced sound, not just the house settling. An hour later, when everyone aside from our group had left, we turned off the lights and sat in the parlor. It was then that we heard a thud upstairs, followed by what sounded like someone walking, and then running, around.

Lou and I turned the lights on, and went upstairs. The rest of the group joined us as we were not looking for ghosts, but making sure that no one was hiding out, trying to stay behind in the house. After a thorough search and finding nothing, we left and set the alarm. Whatever it was making so much noise was apparently not human. Tours continued the next week, including our penultimate night which was on Halloween itself. It was a rainy Friday, and the perfect atmosphere to be scaring people. Little did we know that we were about to be the ones who would be scared.

To preface the following incident, I will say that out of more than 200 videos on YouTube, there is only one where we are scared, flustered, and using profanity out of sheer confusion. This occurred while filming a video on Halloween night, 2014. Prior to shooting the video, we decided to do one quick investigation. During a séance, we began speaking to a spirit who clearly did not want us to be there. This was a new personality; different than anything we had spoken to in the previous year. It was angry and did not like us. It told us as much. The five of us (including Jake, Lou, Hunter, and his friend) kept looking at each other due to a loss for words.

We had sage with us, which we often carry for cleansing and healing purposes—and also protection. Whether or not it really works, it at least makes one feel safe. We felt we needed it that night, as the spirit cursed us out during the séance, the mood became exceptionally dark, and at one point, the wine glass seemed to move slightly on its own without us touching it. We moved the sage to the table, since we were now becoming unnerved by what was happening. The glass started to tremble. The room got cold, which was confirmed by our digital thermometer. We were done.

After spending five exhausting hours doing tours, we decided to call it a night, especially since it seemed like we were not wanted. None of us had ever been scared at the Strauss Mansion before, but there was something different about this. Should we have proceeded and tried to probe further? Maybe, but in the moment, we felt like the right decision was made.

On our way out, we turned off all the lights and set the alarm. We got outside and Hunter pointed out that the second-floor hallway light was on. This could not be so, because I saw Lou shut off that very switch, which is located halfway up the stairs on the first floor. We all really wanted to leave, but we knew we should go turn off the light. I started filming at this point, just in case something paranormal was about to happen. Lou and I went back inside, shut the light, and heard footsteps. We rushed out of the house happy that the deed was done only to see the rest of the group pointing back up to the same second-floor window where the light was seen minutes earlier.

Hunter had noticed something moving in this window, which was in the Victorian bathroom. Lou aimed his flashlight at it, and I did so with my camera. This experience is not well-filmed. I was barely paying attention to the camera on my phone because I was trying to see what was happening with my own eyes. The video was filmed in portrait mode instead of landscape, allowing for only a smaller view to be seen. The rain was drizzling, and we were standing there, staring at something. It was a shadow, but of what? I remarked at the time that it looked like a door slowly closing. In the heat of the moment, we forgot there was no door to that room at all.

I zoomed in on the window, and Lou kept a steady beam with his light, and we ended up capturing a shadow figure moving back and forth in this window. The figure is so dark that the light would not penetrate it. We stood there in disbelief at what we were seeing—the colorful language present in the video is evidence of our genuine shock. The shadow went away, and we left. Lou went home. Jake, Hunter, and I went to IHOP to process what we had just seen. Being at such a restaurant at 2 a.m. might have been the icing on the cake to this insane night, if not just as frightening. We sat at the table in silence.

When I finally did get home, I slept like a baby. I woke up the next morning and went about my day. We had one final night of tours later on. None of us wanted to go upstairs, but we did anyway. When the tours were done, we did not stick around for an investigation, but locked up and headed home. Brett had missed the festivities the night before and came over to my house to hang out. I started telling him the story of what happened and then remembered I shot a video of it. We watched it together, and despite the quality, I was pleasantly surprised to see that I had captured it all. His jaw dropped. Mine dropped again, even though I was there.

The following day was a Sunday, and it was time to clean up the sets and decorations. Brett and I got there early to walk around the house in silence. It was quiet and peaceful. There were no feelings of fear or dread. It was hard to believe our group had just run out of this same place terrified only two days before. I stood in the doorway of that bathroom, looking at the window. It had not dawned on me until then just how remarkable this footage was, not just because of the shadow, but its placement. The bottom of the windowsill is over 5 feet high. The window itself is an additional 5 feet.

This shadow took up the entire window. Was it floating in mid-air or 10 feet tall? Either answer was just as unsettling.

Of course, the next Halloween we were overly excited for what might occur. We set ourselves up for disappointment because of how active the last year had been. There was little to no activity. The Halloween after that was the same, followed by the Halloween after that. We never experienced such visual activity like that ever again nor did we interact with anything as nasty via the séance. It seemed like Halloween itself did not matter, because other days throughout the year could be just as active with noises in the house and getting intelligent responses through the Spirit Box. But as for visual evidence, nothing has ever come close.

The next couple of years were going to be quiet compared to what went on during 2014. I do not know if the house was going through something, or we accidentally stirred something up with all of our events. But such kinds of programs continued and expanded, and while the next few years would see us bringing Patty in as an EVP expert and capturing all kinds of incredible responses, overall the house would be relatively tame.

Such a lull continued until the house shut down during Covid and for about a year after. As we gradually started going into the house more and more, it seemed like the spirits had regained their energy back. Our investigative methods and equipment had also greatly improved. The following chapter will document the second portion of our findings at the Strauss Mansion. What it lacked in visuals, it wholeheartedly made up for in audio, with a series of recordings being so astounding that they might just be the best evidence we have ever documented.

There are no known photographs of the Strauss Mansion from when Adolph and Jeanette lived there, though it is depicted in this early twentieth-century rendering, which was part of a map produced by the town highlighting some of its prominent homes. (*Atlantic Highlands Historical Society*)

The only known photograph of Adolph Strauss (there are none of his wife, Jeanette, that have ever been found), which hangs in the main foyer.

The Strauss Mansion as seen from the edge of Prospect Circle which surrounds it.

The original (and steep) entrance to the Strauss Mansion. Today's "front door" is on the side of the house and requires no climbing.

*Above:* The initials of the home's second owner, Ferdinand Minroth, carved into an outside shingle sometime between 1907 and 1923.

*Right:* The only known personal item left behind by any of the Strauss Mansion's previous nine owners was this fish sauce crate, which I found in the basement in 2017.

*Above:* The sun sets and illuminates the beautiful "A.S" stained glass above what was the original entrance in the foyer. Some have argued that the window would have been facing the other way when Strauss owned the house, so that the letters could be read from the outside. This window and all other stained glass were removed by Fun Wah Chin after the house sold and were made to be purchased back separately by the AHHS. It could have been during this time when the window was put back incorrectly, or maybe it was always this way?

*Left:* It was this high school basketball trophy from the 1920s that managed to become dislodged one night and end up down that hallway to the left.

Many people associate Native American land and artifacts with hauntings and negative energy, but the Strauss Mansion showcases this collection of local arrowheads and tools, and the room it is located in has never seen any terrifying experiences. A photo of a past and beloved AHHS president Paul Boyd watches over the room which is assembled in his honor.

Graffiti from the 1970s in the unrestored third-floor apartment area, including a famous line from a Bob Dylan song and also the name Bob and several others.

The anomaly present in this photograph occurred due to an abnormally long shutter-speed, and it tricked us into thinking we captured a spirit floating above Jake. (*Lou Fligor*)

*Above:* The parlor of the Strauss Mansion where our séance on Halloween night 2014 was held. This is also a great room for setting up "headquarters" during investigations.

*Right:* The window where the shadow was seen moving on Halloween 2014. On a normal night, the only shadow that should be seen is of the curtain, pictured here.

*Left:* The interior of the second-floor bathroom.

*Below:* The non-working Chickering Grand Piano in the parlor that many have heard being played over the years. In one of our own EVPs, it sounded like keys being slammed.

## 12

# THE MOST HAUNTED HOUSE IN NEW JERSEY?
## PART 2

## STRAUSS MANSION MUSEUM, ATLANTIC HIGHLANDS

What happened to us on Halloween night in 2014 may have been a once-in-a-lifetime experience. Not just for what we went through, but also being able to record it on camera. While subsequent Halloweens have not been nearly as active, it was hard to shake what happened from our minds. Nearly every time we investigate, no matter what time of year, we find ourselves outside with a flashlight aimed at that window hoping to either see something move again, or at the very least, attempt to debunk what happened by recreating the same conditions. Of all the paranormal moments I have been present for, this was one that seemed legitimate from the start with no need to debunk. However, after learning our lesson earlier that year, we made sure we would not make the same mistake again.

From right after it happened and even now, we aim the flashlight at the window trying to see if it was something we did which caused a shadow to move. Though Lou was standing still, as evidenced by the angle of the beam, we moved around to different positions trying to see if we could create that same shadow and movement. To this day, it has not happened, and for that reason, I am convinced that what we saw that night was probably the best visual evidence we will ever have.

The following years may not have been as active, but that was because of what we had to compare it to. In the excitement, we set ourselves up for disappointment and temporarily forgot that most haunted locations have nights where nothing happens, or could go through periods of weeks, months, or years with hardly any paranormal activity whatsoever. As time moved on and we headed into 2016, we began to focus more on EVPs, something which we put aside in favor of the instant gratification of the Spirit Box.

Patty came to one of our public investigations as a participant. She was friends with Lou and had an interest in electronic voice phenomena. It was with an old digital recorder (which she refers to as "this rickety little thing") that she started to get the kinds of evidence that we were long missing. She also had the patience and dedication

175

to sit and listen to a four- or five-hour recording just to hopefully hear a chance whisper from beyond the grave.

The first came during one of our séances, when we were asking the name of the spirit we were talking to. Someone joked, "Don't say Francis," which they said was a line from a movie. Almost instantaneously, Patty's recorder captured "Francis," which was an intelligent response, acknowledging what we were speaking about. The next spring, we were doing a private investigation, and during a conversation we were all having about the upcoming town-wide yard sale (there were items we would be selling strewn all over the museum), a female voice was captured saying, "This is nonsense" followed by something unintelligible. It appears that the dead cannot abide by a messy house.

We invited Patty to join us as a team member, not just an occasional participant. I realized that there was possibly so much other evidence we missed out on over the years. Due to the loud noise of the Spirit Box, that made it harder for us to get EVPs when we had our recorders on. In later years, we did more investigating sessions without them, setting our group up in the parlor or library and just asking questions into the darkness, hoping something would be on her recorder when she did her analysis in the following weeks.

On October 13, 2017 (a Friday, no less), we did an investigation following an event. This would be our longest dedicated EVP session, from which Patty was able to pinpoint seven different responses in the span of only a couple of hours. The first was when Joanne asked if Bob ever gets to leave the house or has to remain stuck there. A male voice said, "No you don't." A few minutes later, when Joanne was speaking, there was a frustrated, "Jesus!" being yelled, as if someone was frustrated with us asking so many questions.

The spirits were attracted to Joanne that night because most of the responses were after she had said something. When she whispered that she did not feel anything happening in the house, a voice challenged her with, "What are you supposed to feel?" This was after our detectors noted the temperature dropping in the room from 71 to 65 degrees in just a few minutes. After a couple of unintelligible EVPs, the spirits crisply responded to Joanne's voice one final time, telling her or us to "step upstairs."

Two weeks later, after our tours had wrapped up on October 27, Patrick and I did a midnight walk-through of the Strauss Mansion while he filmed, seeing if anything would happen. As I am standing in the foyer, an orb not only materializes on camera, but moves towards me in a spiral and almost circles me. Upon rewatching this over and over again, it would not appear to be dust given in the direction it moves.

Our investigations, both public and private, continued for the next three years until we were closed during Covid. This was a much-needed break for everyone (including the ghosts), whether we knew it or not. In a way, this recharged us, since the previous years were relatively tame except for some scattered intelligent SB-7 responses and EVPs that are not impactful enough to be written about here. By the time we reopened after Covid, we had also acquired a trap camera, and a REM pod which Jake had lent to us.

As we started to delve right back into where we had left off, we found that the ghosts were almost as active as when I had started investigating in 2014. Jake and I met there one October afternoon in 2020 and went up to the bathroom in the apartment area where Bob allegedly died of an overdose. It had been years since we thought we had spoken to him. I asked a series of questions, one of which was whether the spirits were happy about the lack of action at the museum, and the response through the SB-7 was "two," which happened to be the number of events we had that year due to Covid. Later in the conversation, a female voice says "Bob" and then there was a string of relevant responses including "overdose … on … heroin," "dope," and then "heroin" one more time.

The trap camera ended up being the most valuable piece of equipment we had, because we could leave it overnight or in areas of the house that we were not going to be in. On Halloween in 2020, it was what it did not capture that proved to be interesting. Our group was on the second floor and went downstairs. When we went back up again in an hour or so, we saw a doll on the floor in the same bathroom where the shadow was captured six years earlier. This doll had been located in a small storage room which is right next to the bathroom.

At first, I thought it was a joke or a prank. But we do not do such things to each other during actual investigations. Patty had set the trap camera up on the windowsill facing the doorway where someone would have entered to drop the doll. We pulled up the footage, and we can clearly be seen walking down the hallway to go downstairs. No one enters the bathroom nor tosses the doll in from the hallway. The camera perspective does not reach the floor, so could it have been dragged in?

This was the most activity we had on Halloween since the shadow incident, and something similar was going to occur on the same day two years later in 2022. This time when we went from the first floor up to the second, the "Donna the Dead" animatronic was moved in a different position by the time we returned. We noticed this after I started taking random pictures of the foyer and remembered seeing her standing differently earlier in the night. I asked if anyone had moved her, and no one said they had. Donna has quite an interesting backstory herself, and we refer to her as a "haunted" item and have jokingly suggested that she belongs under glass.

In reality, Donna is a mass-produced Halloween prop owned by Roy and Joanne from the early 1990s that does not work anymore. At one point, her eyes glowed green, she moved back and forth, and let out this awful wailing sound. Today, unable to move or talk, she still manages to frighten people. Visitors to the museum for events in October have sworn they saw her move and glow, only to find out that she cannot be plugged in any longer.

It was this same figure that became dislodged in the Tower Room decades ago and nearly burned the Strauss Mansion to the ground. It is a figure that Joanne lent to the Atlantic Cinemas in 2021, and late one night after setting her up, the theater's alarm was tripped hours after closing. The owner at the time, who was also a private investigator, arrived at the theater armed, turned down a hallway and saw a shadowy figure with long hair highlighted and backlit by the sinister red glow of an emergency exit sign. It was Donna. He drew his gun and nearly shot her. Bullet holes would have only added to her provenance.

Perhaps the items have more of an effect on paranormal activity than the house itself. There are thousands of pieces inside the twenty-one rooms of the Strauss Mansion Museum. Each has their own story, which may be the cause for another book. While Donna comes and goes every fall, the rest are on permanent display. Hardly any of them are original to previous owners. Everything has been loaned or donated over the last four decades since the building became a museum. For people who believe that items can be haunted or have spiritual attachments, this answers the question as to how it would be possible for one single location to have so many different personalities.

A good portion of them have been acquired through donations after someone has passed away. This is especially the case when it comes to antique furniture or artwork, where family members processing the collection of someone's estate might not know what to do with such large pieces. They frequently come to this museum. Then there are the fifty or so items that were transferred to the AHHS following the closure of the Spy House Museum Corporation. In examining release forms from July and August 1997, the Strauss Mansion received lanterns, lamps, paintings, Victorian greeting cards, a spool bed, antique vacuum cleaner, hat holders, mannequins and dress forms, drink pitchers, tools, a crib, and more.

The list shows most of them "on loan," but since no museum ever reopened, some of these might still be present. In talking to board member Bette VanDeventer (the longest-serving and only one currently who was active when this transfer happened), she explained that a lot of them were returned to their previous owners over the years, but perhaps not all were ever claimed. That will be my next quest, in trying to track down which items from that legendary location are still there.

The two years in between these later Halloween incidents saw our trap camera positioned at the base of the steps in the foyer capturing moments when we least expected it. At 5:38 a.m. on December 20, 2020, a door was heard slamming in the audio of this camera. There were two distinct sounds, one of the knob itself being grabbed, and then the slam which followed about three seconds later. There was no one in the house, and despite the potential for settling noises or vibrations caused by outside traffic, this clearly was a door being physically shut. Our group showed up later that week to attempt to replicate the noise. There are sixty-nine doors in the house, but thankfully by the time we slammed the one between the parlor and breakfast room, we determined that was the closest sound. We had about thirty to go. The trap camera only records when it is triggered, and it was already filming when the noise was heard, so something caused it to turn on. What this was does not appear on camera.

Three days later, with the camera still in the same spot, a mist materialized and swirled around in front of it at 11:02 p.m. We had been in the house earlier that night testing out the doors, but we were out of there by then. It could not have been smoke, or the fire alarm would have gone off. It also was not breath or air of some kind, since no one was inside the building and such a manifestation did not occur again the entire night (or before or since).

February 27, 2021 would see us be presented with our best ever audio evidence, which may be more remarkable than the shadow figure. A few of us had gotten together to do some work in the archives room since the museum was going to be opening in a couple of months and we were on the hunt for items we could use in new exhibits. This night did not see us do any investigating. We were still wearing masks and trying to keep socially distanced as best as we could. Patty set the camera up in the same place in the foyer while we were upstairs. In the video, we can be seen coming down the stairs to leave for the night, but a voice is captured screaming while this is happening.

Patty came down first, then two others, one of whom stopped to look in the mirror. My voice is heard chatting with someone upstairs, and then over all of it was an incredibly loud, "Get … out!" None of us heard this at the time, making it a classic

EVP picked up by the trap camera. This burst of energy was so remarkable in that it was simultaneously captured on Patty's digital recorder which she was wearing around her neck. But there was more. Following those two words, there appeared to be a bang followed by more unintelligible words. We posted the trap camera footage which was only thirty seconds before it stops filming and then starts again. By the time it started up, the rest of whatever this ghost was saying was missed. But we had the other recorder as well.

While the "get out" is faint, the rest of it picks up where the trap camera left off. Patty was in the parlor, with this activity seeming to happen directly above us. In her audio recording, we can hear her begin to ask where something is as she is starting to put her equipment away. The bang is much louder here, almost sounding like a gunshot, while the voice seems to scream in agony right after that. There are unintelligible words following this scream, which are spoken in distress. We do not know what the bang was. Did I shut a door upstairs and unknowingly cause it? I do not remember, because such an action would not have been noteworthy, but it is doubtful that I would have slammed a door like that. The bang could have been on the other side and therefore inaudible to us.

There is no record of anyone being shot or killed in the house, but if you view the footage, you may agree that it sounds like a gunshot. It is so very important that we have two recordings here of the same incident because it helps us construct a timeline. Based on the trap camera alone, it would seem that the ghosts were telling us to "get out." But the second recording leads me to believe this is not the case. Much like the "choke to kill" sound bite in the basement from 2014, this might have been an argument or altercation occurring in their dimension between spirits. A man screams at someone to get out, there is a loud bang and some undetermined physical activity, a scream in pain, and then distressed speaking. In human terms, that sounds like a fight to me, and what are ghosts but simply former humans?

When lecturing, I often use the phrase "Holy Grail" to describe the type of evidence we are hoping to find as we conduct these investigations across multiple locations. This may be it, along with the video of the shadow moving in the bathroom window. And while that video will always be one for the ages, upon further reflection, I have the feeling that this audio just might be more important. The amount of energy it took this spirit to yell and the ensuing actions and screaming is really of a different magnitude.

Over the years, we have had ghosts say many things to us (and each other), and not all of it pleasant. We have been greeted politely, cursed out, questioned, introduced to, heard arguments between spirits, and a lot of other responses with no apparent meaning, but this blew me away. It takes a lot to do that. With our hundreds of pieces of evidence, in more than a decade, I have only been truly floored three times: the Proprietary House in 2012, Halloween 2014, and this random chilly February night in 2021.

Regardless of the location, you never know what will happen when you show up for an investigation, or if you are not doing any paranormal research at all. This was just a normal night trying to set up for an exhibit. You also never know what you will find when you return home and start to look through your pictures and video, and hopefully have the patience to sift through hours of audio.

At the end of 2022, with our recorders running, as we sat quietly in the parlor during an EVP session, the first three notes of "Lullaby" were heard with our own ears. It astounded everyone in the room, in an almost unconscionable manner, because where could that sound have come from? No one was on their phones and there is no object within the Strauss Mansion which could have caused the music to play. It also did not sound digital. Three days later, I went back with Patrick and Christian to do a daytime SB-7 session and while it was incredibly active with intelligent responses, we came no closer to finding out why "Lullaby" would be playing. There are several antique baby carriages located throughout the house. Is someone attached to one of them, be it a mother or an infant? It will remain one of the many mysteries at this haunted location.

The investigations continue to this very day at the Strauss Mansion, for our group and many others who can rent the location and check it out for themselves. Some of them manage to come up with similar interactions between spirits we have talked to over the years, and others find entirely new information. The years 2022 and 2023 saw the most uses by different groups than ever before, and most of them were drawn to a small antique school desk which is displayed in the Tower Room. These groups, unconnected to each other, have all come up with the idea that there is specifically a little girl attached to the desk. This is something that we had never noticed in our hundreds of investigations, and why it is important for different groups to investigate the same location, because as we do our digging, we are only given fragments—the pieces to a giant puzzle. It takes more than one person or one group to tell the story.

As I was finishing this book, a group at the Strauss Mansion in the fall of 2023 brought with them a newer version of the Spirit Box which filters out the static and makes it easier to hear the actual responses. They demonstrated this in front of a group, and over the course of a few minutes, the names "Adolph" and "Jeanette" were heard. I smiled when I heard this, because I did not think we ever spoke to the Strausses, or that they were even present (much like trying to reach Franklin at the Proprietary House). Or maybe it was not them at all, but other ghosts who simply knew about their existence.

At the end of the day, with so many thoughts going through my mind during these investigations, I wonder what the ghosts truly think of us. That these entities who once lived and breathed like us and inhabited these houses are now seeing them either be lived in by others or used as a public museum, and have to deal with people coming in trying to speak to them. Are they happy? Annoyed? Or maybe both? We have to remind ourselves that ghosts were just like us and capable of the same emotions and feelings. They can range from happy to sad, and also angry, much like we can.

We try to never lose sight of the history of a location for this reason, in trying to not only capture evidence but also see a window into the past and communicate with someone who lived before us. The Strauss Mansion's many owners over the years, the architecture of the house, and the items accumulated since it became a museum all factor into this investigating. My group and I have been extremely fortunate to be given such access to this location, and it is never something that I never take for granted.

Roy and Joanne's animatronic figure "Donna the Dead," which can be seen on display at the Strauss Mansion every October. But what about the strange occurrences she brings? A coincidence or is she herself haunted?

Inside the tower on the third floor. It was that pole that Donna was strapped to, and became dislodged from, almost causing a fire. The small hole in the floor was where it started to burn.

A mist materializes in front of the trap camera when no one was in the house. (*Patty Bickauskas*)

*Opposite page:* It was by that lamp on the table in the foyer that the trap camera was placed for our series of incredible captures.

*Above:* This desk was once used at Atlantic Highlands Elementary School. While our group has not noticed any activity around it, others have claimed there is a spirit of a little girl attached to it.

*Below:* An antique baby carriage and crib on display in a small nursery room.

# EPILOGUE

We are lucky to live in an area that not only has so much history and haunted locations but has such places that can be visited by the public. There are more investigations of locations that I have conducted in places not in this book, but some are not public and accessible. I kept the locations featured here to ones that anyone can investigate or at least visit for themselves and perhaps start their own journey.

The Strauss Mansion is open every Sunday from May through November for free self-guided tours. It is also available for paranormal rentals. The Proprietary House is open on select Sundays for paid tours, with Wednesday openings available by request. Fort Hancock and the Halyburton Memorial on Sandy Hook, Deep Cut Gardens, Poricy Park where Joseph Murray's murder occurred, and Hudson Springs are all located in public parks which are open 365 days a year. The Dempsey House is on private property but can be viewed closely from the street. Whipporwill is a public road, but almost all of the surrounding woods which is so alluring is private property which you cannot trespass on. Bay View Cemetery is open daily until 4 p.m., the Thrift Shop has limited hours of operation on Wednesdays (the manager Roseanne is more than happy to discuss the property's history), and the movie theater and Atlantic House restaurant are in business with regular hours. The Spy House is typically not open to the public but does hold special events throughout the year, though they rarely address anything other than local environmental topics.

And so I invite you to explore these locations for yourself, and if you are so interested, check out the videos that accompany many of the moments discussed so you can see and analyze for yourself. If you are still reading, I hope you enjoyed the book. I also hope the paranormal skeptics out there managed to find enough history embedded within these pages that it still kept you interested. This geographic region has something for everyone, and as we have seen with certain time periods, the truth can sometimes be stranger than fiction—and the living can be scarier than the dead.

# REFERENCES

## PRINT AND INTERNET


"1705, Dec 19-21, Privateer Castle Del Rey, Grounds/Breaks-up, Sandy Hook, NJ," *US Deadly Events*, n.d.

"A Triangle of Land: A History of the Site, Founding, and Progress of Brookdale Community College", Brookdale Community College, 2016.

Adelberg, M. S., *The American Revolution in Monmouth County: The Theatre of Spoil and Destruction* (United States: The History Press, 2010)

"Admiralty Acknowledges Kindness in Burying Bodies of Officers Frozen in 1783," *New York Times*, September 6, 1908

Alexander, L., "The Dead Actress Spoke to Me: The Strange and Suspicious Story of Charlotte Behrens Mantell," *Genealogy Today*, July 20, 2001

"A Walking Tour of Deep Cut Gardens," *Monmouth County Park System*, n.d.

"Bay View Cemetery," Find a Grave, October 8, 2000

Bell, M. L., *I Remember* (New Jersey: Atlantic Highlands Historical Society, 1986)

Blackwell, J., *Notorious New Jersey* (New Jersey: Rivergate Books, 2007)

Boyd, P. D., *Atlantic Highlands: From Lenape Camps to Bayside Town* (United States: Arcadia Publishing, 2004)

Boyd, P. D., *Robert Mantell and Brucewood* (New Jersey: Atlantic Highlands Historical Society, 2008)

Boyd, P. D., and Poll, L., *The Strauss Mansion Tour Guide* (New Jersey: Atlantic Highlands Historical Society, 2008)

Boyd, P. D., *The Strauss Family, the Strauss Mansion, and Their Many Lives* (New Jersey: Atlantic Highlands Historical Society, 2007)

Bulliet, C. J., *Robert Mantell's Romance* (Boston: J.W. Luce, 1918)

Carino, J., "Captain Kidd, Blackbeard and Buried Pirate Treasure at the Bayshore? Truth vs. Tales," *Asbury Park Press*, October 31, 2022

Carino, J., "Mafia Kingpin Vito Genovese Lived in These Monmouth County Homes," *Asbury Park Press*, June 23, 2022

"Chas. L. Duvale Dead: Was Found Asphyxiated by Gas in his Kitchen," *The Atlantic Highlander*, January 9, 1918

"Chapel Hill Rear Range Lighthouse," *Lighthouse Friends*, n.d.

"Charlotte Behrens Mantell," Find a Grave, April 20, 2012

"Conover Beacon Lighthouse," Lighthouse Friends, n.d.

"Deep Cut Gardens," Monmouth County Park System, n.d.

"Dempsey Pump House," New Jersey Historic Trust, n.d.

Franklin, B., Last Will and Testament, 1789

Frasca, D., *King of Crime: The Story of Vito Genovese, Mafia Czar* (United States: Crown Publishers, 1959)

"Fund Drive Starts for Hudson Spring," *Asbury Park Press*, n.d.

Grodeska, J., "Lawyers, Guns, & Money: The Alexander Lillien Story Part Three: Smugglers Blues," *Jersey Shore Scene*, January 31, 2022

Grodeska, J., "The Lost Tomb at Sandy Hook," *Jersey Shore Scene*, February 11, 2020

Hawarden, F. Z., "Hudson Springs," *The Daily Register*, January 6, 1975

Hawk, T., "Was N.J.'s Spy House One of the Most Haunted Spots in the Country? That's Up for Debate," NJ.Com, November 2, 2019

"Henry Hudson Springs," Historical Marker Database, 2020

Herget, A., "Police ID Man Found in Pool," *Asbury Park Press*, December 26, 2006

"High Cost Shelves Saving of Spring," *Asbury Park Press*, n.d.

"Historic Spring May Be Restored," *Asbury Park Press*, January 19, 1975

Hodges, G. R., *Slavery and Freedom in the Rural North: African Americans in Monmouth County, New Jersey, 1665–1865* (United States: Rowman & Littlefield, 1997)

Husted, H., "Abigail Sharp: New Jersey's One Witch," New Jersey State Library, October 18, 2021

Izenberg, J., "Haskell 2019: Here's the Story Behind the Guy Who Made Monmouth Park's Million-Dollar Race Possible," NJ.Com, July 16, 2019

"Killed in Street Fight," *Red Bank Register*, October 24, 1923

Koutnik, E., "Spy House Now Part of Bayshore Park," *Independent*, August 13, 1997

Leonard, T. H., *From Indian Trail to Electric Rail* (New Jersey: Atlantic Highlands Journal, 1923)

Linderoth, M., *Prohibition on the North Jersey Shore: Gangsters on Vacation* (United States: The History Press, 2010)

Lopez, R., "New Life for an Old Mansion," *New York Times*, September 18, 1977

Mandeville, E., *The Story of Middletown: The Oldest Settlement in New Jersey: An Exact Reprint* (United States: Academy Press, 1972)

"Marie Booth Russell Mantell," Find a Grave, November 7, 2013

Moon, E. N., "Odd Going-On at the Spy House," *New York Times*, January 24, 1993

Moran, M., and Sceurman, M., "Hunting for the Buried Treasure of Captain Kidd," *Weird N.J.*, June 1, 2021

Moran, M., and Sceurman, M., "Is the Spy House 'The Most Haunted House in America'?" *Weird N.J.*, November 3, 2014

Moran, M., and Sceurman, M., "Legends of the Dempsey House," *Weird N.J.*, September 12, 2014

Moran, M., and Sceurman, M., "The Ghostly Glow of Green Light Cemetery," *Weird N.J.*, November 6, 2021

Moran, M., and Sceurman, M., "Whipporwill Valley and Cooper Roads: Middletown's Scariest Byways," *Weird N.J.*, September 5, 2014

Moss Jr., G. H., *Nauvoo to the Hook: The Iconography of a Barrier Beach* (New Jersey: Jersey Close Press, 1964)

Mullins, D., *Victorian Actors and Actresses in Review* (London: Greenwood Press, 1983)

"National Register of Historic Places Inventory - Nomination Form: Seabrook-Wilson House," United States Department of the Interior, National Park Service, October 29, 1974

Neidlinger, G., "The Heritage of the Bayshore: Spy House and Shoal Harbor Museum," Spy House Museum Corporation, n.d.

Neidlinger, G., "The Spy House Museum," Spy House Museum Corporation, n.d.

"No Suspect in Haskell Arson Probe," *Red Bank Register*, July 26, 1966

"Private Playground at Leonardo," *The Monmouth Press*, August 7, 1914

Randall, W., *A Little Revenge: Benjamin Franklin and His Son* (Boston: Little, Brown & Co., 1984)

Release Forms from the Spy House Museum Corporation to the Atlantic Highlands Historical Society, 1997

Robert, S., "New York's Coldest Case: A Murder 400 Years Old," *New York Times*, September 4, 2009

"Robert Bruce Mantell, Jr.," Find a Grave, May 22, 2003

"Robert Bruce Mantell, Sr.," Find a Grave, July 18, 2002

Rockwell, C., *The Catskill Mountains and the Region Around* (New York: Taintor Brothers and Co., 1867)

"Seabrook-Wilson House," New Jersey Historic Trust, n.d.

"Séance Held at the Spy House," Spy House Museum Corporation, November 6, 1975

Shipwreck Database 020423, New Jersey Maritime Museum

"The Bootlegger Era: Prohibition in New Jersey," Monmouth County Archives, 2013

"The Henry Hudson Monument," *New York Times*, September 21, 1891

"The Matawan Shark Attack: A Deadly Day in 1916," *Yesterday's America*, n.d.

"The Story of Henry Hudson Spring," Atlantic Highlands Historical Society, 1977

"The War Years, 1776–1783: The Spy House," *Tel-News*, 1984

"Thomas W. Bailiff v. New Jersey State Parole Board," *JUSTIA U.S Law*, February 8, 2017

Thorn, J., "Henry Hudson and the Half Moon, 1609," *Gotham History*, May 12, 2015

Unidentified Shipwreck Database 013119, New Jersey Maritime Museum

Untitled, *The Monmouth Press*, October 2, 1914

Van Develde, E., "Myth vs. Reality: Whipporwill Valley Road and the Nancy Clark Murder," *Rumson-Fair Haven Patch*, August 11, 2012

"Vito and Anna Genovese Move to Middletown," *Monmouth Timeline*, n.d.

"Vito Genovese Asserts Himself on the Monmouth County Docks," Monmouth Timeline, n.d.

Wallace, H., "The Haskell Hunt: A Piece of History in My Backyard," The Timid Rider, 2017

Weintraub, S., *George Washinton's Christmas Farewell* (New York: Free Press, 2007)

"Weird NJ: Deadly Tale of Henry Hudson Springs," *Asbury Park Press*, March 12, 2017

"Welcome to the Bayshore Waterfront Park Activity Center," Monmouth County Park System, n.d.

Youmans, J., "Spirits of the Spy House," *Coast Magazine*, 1988

Zimmer, D., "Was Henry Hudson's Shipmate Buried in NJ 410 Years Ago? Yes Says One Man," *Bergen Record*, May 22, 2019

Zimmer, R., "Spy House: The Story Behind the Ghost Stories," *Asbury Park Press*, October 21, 2016.

Zink, C. W., *Brookdale Farm in Thompson Park*, Friends of the Monmouth County Park System, 2016

## PREVIOUS WORKS BY THE AUTHOR REFERENCED

"Exploring 'Haunted' Whipporwill Road," *Caggiano's Corner*, June 22, 2010

*Ghost Hunting Confidential: Investigating Strauss Mansion* (New Jersey: Atlantic Highlands Historical Society, 2014)

"Governor William Franklin and the Price of Dissent," *Garden State Legacy*, 2013

"Return to Spy House Confirms Sighting From Previous Visit," *Caggiano's Corner*, May 11, 2010

"Spy House Documents and Folklore," *Caggiano's Corner*, September 22, 2015

"The Invented History of the Spy House," *Garden State Legacy*, 2014

"Twenty Minutes at the Spy House was More than Enough," *Caggiano's Corner*, May 9, 2010

## YOUTUBE VIDEOS REFERENCED

"Aftermath of an Incredible Incident on Halloween Night," *Ghosts on the Coast*, November 1, 2020.

"A Strange Mist Materializes in the Strauss Mansion Foyer," *Ghosts on the Coast*, December 23, 2020

"Brookdale Paranormal Camp Investigation Day 3," *Ghosts on the Coast*, July 8, 2016

"Evidence Discussion: Strauss Mansion Second Floor Bathroom Window," *Ghosts on the Coast*, November 1, 2015

"Evidence Review: 'Get Up...Get Out'," *Ghosts on the Coast*, November 26, 2017

"Extended Audio Clip of 'Get Out' and Explanation," *Ghosts on the Coast*, March 1, 2021

"Ghostly Lullaby at the Strauss Mansion," *Ghosts on the Coast*, January 1, 2023

"Group Spirit Box Session in Original Section of Spy House," *Haunted Travels*, February 8, 2014

"Halloween at Port Monmouth, NJ's Spy House," *Ghosts on the Coast*, November 1, 2018

"Haunted History: Ghosts of the Halyburton Tragedy," *Ghosts on the Coast*, January 25, 2023

"Haunted History: The Curse of Hudson Springs," *Ghosts on the Coast*, February 15, 2023

"Haunted History: The Godfather's Garden," *Ghosts on the Coast*, April 15, 2023

"Haunted History: The Legends of Whipporwill Road," *Ghosts on the Coast*, March 15, 2023

"Historian Tom Burke Discusses the History of Rose Hill Cemetery," *Haunted Travels*, March 8, 2014

"Listen to a Door Slam on its Own at the Strauss Mansion," *Ghosts on the Coast*, December 21, 2020

"Middletown NJ's 'Green Light Cemetery' SB-7 Session," *Ghosts on the Coast*, June 23, 2019

"Midnight at the Mansion," *Ghosts on the Coast*, October 28, 2017

"Past Evidence: Strauss Mansion Shadow Movement on Halloween," *Ghosts on the Coast*, October 31, 2015

"Seven EVP Recordings," *Ghosts on the Coast*, October 23, 2017

"Spirit Box Session in Strauss Mansion Basement," *Haunted Travels*, January 5, 2014

"Spirit Box Session Near 'Abigail's Window' at the Spy House," *Haunted Travels*, February 9 2014

"Strauss Mansion EVP Recording," *Ghosts on the Coast*, November 26, 2016

"The Best EVP Recording We Have Captured So Far," *Ghosts on the Coast*, May 4, 2017

"Trap Camera Captures Ghostly Scream 'Get Out!'," *Ghosts on the Coast*, February 28, 2021

"Trap Camera Perspective for Halloween Experience," *Ghosts on the Coast*, November 2, 2020

"Who's the Baby?" *Ghosts on the Coast*, January 16, 2023

# ABOUT THE AUTHOR

**Greg Caggiano** is an award-winning historian and lecturer who has spent most of his life in the Bayshore area of Monmouth County, New Jersey. Since 2014, he has been an instructor for Brookdale Community College's Lifelong Learning department and lectures at libraries, museums, and organizations across the state on a variety of American and world history subjects.

He has served on the boards of two museums: the Proprietary House from 2010–2013 and the Atlantic Highlands Historical Society, housed at the Strauss Mansion Museum, from 2014–2022. This gave him unrivaled access to two incredibly haunted locations and sparked an interest in investigating the paranormal with a historical spin and also examining established myths and legends for authenticity.

He takes this approach to writing and lectures as he feels that paranormal investigating is an important window into studying the past. For that reason, even skeptics have enjoyed Greg's presentation of paranormal evidence and investigations into local lore. As a lifelong believer in volunteering and giving back to the community, Greg and his paranormal team have fundraised tens of thousands of dollars over the years for historic sites.